TERMINAL 4

AN ENTREPRENEURS JOURNEY FROM BICYCLE TO BUSINESS CLASS

Terminal 4 by Nilesh Makwana is a fabulous tale of a lifelong learner, an adventurer, an entrepreneur and intrepid traveller. The account of his life is as entertaining and engaging as it is motivating. From being a student with a poor academic track record in small town India to becoming an entrepreneur who has travelled the world, won multiple awards and added tremendous value to the community, Nilesh's story of perseverance, passion, grit, self-belief and never-say-die spirit will surely be inspirational to all who read it. I loved the summary of life lessons at the end of each chapter. Wishing Nilesh all the best in his journey hereon. If this account is anything to go by, I am sure many new adventures and accolades await!"

— *Preeti Vyas*

President & CEO, Amar Chitra Katha Pvt. Ltd.

"The book is inspirational and motivational. It's well written, witty, and racy. Nilesh shares his life's experiences which are relatable, practical and easy to follow. Terminal 4 provides a safe landing not only for foreign students but has life lessons for everyone, and is a must read for young entrepreneurs."

— *Dr Mukesh Batra*

Founder & Chairman Emeritus, Dr Batra's™ Group

An enjoyable story of optimism, perseverance and the importance of making the most of every opportunity. A great read for international students, migrants and for us all.

— Annie Fogarty

Executive Chairperson, Fogarty Foundation

"The book is indeed a must read for new arrivals to WA, students, and migrants alike. In fact, I think everyone can take something away from reading it, and to be inspired by your message of active citizenship and leading with karma."

— Hari Sethi

CEO & Founder, National Institute of Technology (NIT) Australia

"You have come so far, and in such an interesting and inspirational manner, all of which is conveyed with eloquence and passion. Your values, character, story all come through here, and it is wonderful to share it with international students and other potential readers."

— Robert Wood

Creative Director, Centre for Stories

"The book can be read by everyone as it is a wonderful book with lots of life experience. I think this book would really motivate young people who leave their home country and move to a completely new world. This book can show them that bad times do not stay and with struggle and hard work comes success and satisfaction."

— Karan Joshi

Director & CEO, Aussizz Group

"I was brought back to my own migration days, and by reading about your journey I remembered many things I had forgotten about from my own big move from Europe to Australia."

— Alberto Tassone

President, Stanley College

"I like the blend of humour and Nilesh's raw experiences."

— Krishna Karangiya

Project Officer, Kaleidoscope Initiative

"I am an international student and have gone through a lot of struggles. When I was reading the book there were places where I felt like 'this is my life as well.' This book made me realise I have so much left to achieve, and with the author's insights and messages I feel better equipped to succeed in this foreign land."

— Imran Rashid

International Student, Australia

"I am not much of a book reader, but this book had so many real-life experiences that I could relate to, and it kept me tied to it. I cannot believe that I completed the whole book in one sitting! It is very engaging and every page you turn has something to offer and it kept making me want to read more."

— Marcia De Oliveira

Business Development Manager, NIT Australia

"The best thing about this book was the honesty and integrity in the story."

— Dev Kumar

International Student, Australia

"With this book you get a front seat on an adventurous journey that is about struggle, hard work, and persistence. The quote before each chapter set the tone of what is to come beautifully and the key takeaways after every chapter left me with an even better understanding of my business partner. In this book, Nilesh doesn't hide or smooth over any challenges or failures he faced in his life, but gracefully shares them with us all to learn from."

— Vincent Lam

Principal Consultant, illuminance Solutions

"This story, of a small-town boy who repeatedly failed in school and then went on to become a global, award-winning entrepreneur, is told in simple language, peppered with pithy quotes and insightful takeaways. Engagingly written, with candour and humour, this is an inspiring tale and one that I would recommend being read by everyone who wants to understand what it takes to succeed in a complex and unforgiving world."

— Menka Shivdasani

Poet and Writer, Mumbai

— Des Kumar

— Monika Srivastava

Poet and Writer, Mumbai

TERMINAL 4

AN ENTREPRENEUR'S JOURNEY FROM BICYCLE TO BUSINESS CLASS

NILESH MAKWANA

Popular Prakashan
www.popularprakashan.com

Published by
Harsha Bhatkal for
Popular Prakashan Pvt. Ltd.
301, Mahalaxmi Chambers
22, Bhulabhai Desai Road
Mumbai 400026
info@popularprakashan.com

First Published 2022

(4542)
ISBN 978-81-956688-2-3

Disclaimer: The events are portrayed to the best of the author's memory. While all the stories in this book are true, some names and identifying details have been changed to protect the privacy of the people involved. The views and opinions expressed in this work are the author's own and the facts are as reported by the author, and the publisher is in no way liable for the same.

Cover and layout design: Lene Makwana

Typesetting: Anjali Sawant

Printed In India
by Shree J Printers Pvt. Ltd.
1416, Sadashiv Peth
Pune 411030

Contents

Acknowledgements

This book is dedicated to my parents, my family and Phiroze Uncle and Maneck Aunty, without whom I would not be who I am today.

A special thank you to Katie McDonald and my wife Lene for all your hard work, and to my colleagues and second family at illuminance Solutions and my business partner Vincent Lam for all their support, faith and patience.

Thank you to every teacher and lecturer that I had throughout my life, from failing school in India to receiving distinctions at university in the UK and in Australia. I never was an easy student, and I am grateful for the patience and sometimes lack of patience that you all showed me. It all served a purpose.

A special greeting to my friends from all over the world who helped me with what I found most difficult while writing this book; choosing the title and finalising the cover design. Without you this book would never have seen the light of day.

Thank you to all the international students, young entrepreneurs and migrants who contact me daily for my help and support. You are my inspiration. I also dedicate this book to you, my reader, and to everyone who may have been or perhaps will be finding themselves in similar situations to mine.

A big thank you to my publisher Mr Harsha Bhatkal and his team at Popular Prakashan for making my dream come true, and to Dr Mukesh Batra who brought us together. It is true what they say, it takes a village to raise a child. You don't achieve anything by yourself in life, and there is always someone who will guide you, support you and sometimes even hold your hand. Thank you to everyone who has played a part in my life so far, big or small, and to everyone yet to play a part. You are my village, and I am grateful to every single one of you for the love, encouragement, kindness and concern you have showered on me. This book is yours just as much as it is mine.

Introduction

"Failure is not the opposite of success – it's a part of it."

– William Ritter

My father celebrated every time I failed in school as a young boy. In India, it's customary to bring out sweets and delicious foods on the day children bring home their report cards from school. This is of course to celebrate their hard work and good marks. However, in my case, the news I brought home every time was often accompanied by a letter from the principal suggesting that my parents find me a tutor or even informing them that I had failed in every subject. My father still brought out the ice cream, as my brother and sisters also brought their report cards home on the same day. But their cards weren't as red as mine, and they deserved to be treated for their good work.

When I was young, I had neither the time for, nor the slightest interest in school. I was the worst student - if you could even call me a 'student,' for that would suggest I was studying... or at least attending school to begin with. From a very young age I had a flair for business and while my friends were playing ball games or hopscotch during recess, I did what I thought was more fun: selling stickers and pens. When I grew a little older, I got a bicycle and upscaled my business to selling electric sandwich makers and other appliances to nearly every household in my neighbourhood, after school, and sometimes even during the time I was supposed to be in school. It goes without saying that I failed school, not once but several times.

Little did I know back then that I would be a 'student' in all forms of the word throughout my life, and that education would be my key to unlocking opportunities that would take me all over the world and eventually, to a place in Western Australia called Perth, or according to the First Nations' Noongar people, Mooro in the Whadjuk region.

I'm a long way from my hometown, Rajkot in India, where my journey began. But there's no place I'd rather be. As you will soon find out, that's a big call considering all the places I have visited. From bustling cities like London and New York, to the snowy alps of Switzerland and sprawling mountains of Rio de Janeiro, I'd choose Perth every single time.

If you're asking yourself, 'where is 'Perth?' I will tell you that it is the most isolated capital city in the world, and a place I like to call Heaven on Earth. Located on the west coast of Australia, it's a place that welcomes migrants like myself, supports international students and foreign workers, and those who have the courage to give something Aussies like to call a 'fair go'. The idea of a 'fair go' embraces the ideas of mutual respect, tolerance, compassion, and equality of opportunity for all. For that, I am forever grateful, as it is what has got me to where I am today.

Sometimes, when I am cycling along the South Perth foreshore on one of my weekend rides, and my feet push down on the pedals of my bicycle, I am transported back to the 1980s, to the streets of my hometown Rajkot. I recall the countless days of huffing and puffing my way from door to door, where I was instantly recognisable in the neighbourhood thanks to my trusty - but very rusty - red bike. My little sister often hitched a ride on the back, holding onto my shoulders.

If it had not been for Perth, I may never have been able to co-run a successful, social impact driven business, or connect with so many people - friendly locals as well as migrants and international students - all of them entrepreneurial spirits.

And that is what brought me to putting this book together for you. Over the years I have been invited to give talks and presentations at universities, business meetings and community groups, and they all ask me to do the same thing; to share my journey. I still pinch myself sometimes, it's not bad for a guy who dropped out of school or failed so many times. I have studied in London and in Perth, and have met incredible people, like the CEO of Microsoft, Satya Nadella, and Ajay Banga, the president of Mastercard. I have eaten acai bowls with Michael Jackson's former surgeon in Brazil, had dinner at Prime Minister Modi's table, been detained in a Mexican airport holding cell, discovered the joy that is Nutella by trying it for the first time, while whizzing through Switzerland on a train, and I have built a business from the ground up, only to lose everything and start again. But starting again brought more success than I could have ever imagined.

So how did I do it?

There's really no secret or magic behind it and I will share everything with you in this book. I never won awards at school - no trophies, ribbons, or merit certificates (I did, however, eventually win a student election... more on that later), but the awards certainly flowed later in life: in recent years I have been named a Gold Disruptor in the Chief Experience Officer (CXO) Disruptor of the Year category at the Australian Computer Society Digital Disruptor Awards, I received the City of Perth award at the Business News 40under40 Awards, and I have also become an Australian citizen. The success extends to 19-, the company I now run with my business partner, Vincent Lam, which came on to the global stage when it won the inaugural Global Microsoft Partner for Social Impact in 2019. But my favourite highlight is that I have been a lecturer for Masters' students at Edith Cowan University. For many years I never even thought I'd finish school, so as a drop-out and failure, who was I to teach?

Now, it's great to look back on these achievements, and life's most joyous moments, but they did not come without struggle, hard work and lots of learning. I have also taken big risks, like leaving my family and everything I'd ever known in India.

Trying to build a new life somewhere else has many similarities to trying to build a business - you'll cry, laugh and cry again, get homesick (either for a place or a previous job with a stable, secure income). I have felt the pressure of putting everything on the line and wanting to make my father and my family proud. I also wanted to give up many times. But these are the same obstacles that most established businesses and people have faced during their journey before making it to the top of the mountain of success. Often they fall down the mountain, only to pick themselves up again.

When the COVID-19 pandemic hit in 2020, the world was forced to pause, reflect, and reset. We all had to find ways to pick ourselves up again, and to keep going, no matter what. This book is part of my reset. I want to help and motivate more international students, migrants and founders of start-ups, who may have left a small town in pursuit of bigger and better things in a new country and who will face the same challenges I did; navigating language barriers, visa restrictions and relationships, and having to work very hard to reach that 'light at the end of the tunnel'.

There was a time not long ago when I had no money and no job and was almost forced to leave this beautiful country. I had lost almost everything, but I was lucky to still have my marriage and the support of my life partner, Lene and my family back home. I also had determination - that's one thing no one else can take away from you - only you can take it away. Sometimes it takes losing almost everything to truly appreciate what you have. I already knew this but maybe 2020 has made that clearer. Our time on this planet is short, so what legacy do you want to leave behind?

If you are looking for something to give you that little push you need to take the first steps towards your own big dream, I invite you to step into my world. Maybe you feel trapped, or scared and overwhelmed - not sure what the future holds.

You could be a student or an immigrant, just like me, or simply someone with business ideas.

Whoever you are - it's nice to meet you.

My name is Nilesh Makwana. I am a Hindu Indian migrant, international student, and entrepreneur with a passion for social impact, who is only just getting started. Turn the page and come on a journey with me. It might just provide the little spark you need to embark on a journey of your own.

Chapter 1

Cows Make Great Teachers

"One of the huge mistakes people make is that they try to force an interest on themselves. You don't choose your passions; your passions choose you."

– Jeff Bezos

My story starts in Rajkot, my hometown in India. When I think back on those days, I remember the cows.

Every day, one particular cow would find her way into our front garden, stick her brown head through the window and moo to let us know she was ready for a snack. Then once content, off she went, back down our driveway through the gates, into the world, weaving her way through the chaos that is traffic in India, acting as if she didn't have a care in the world. She probably didn't, and cows in my country are left to do their own thing.

I also liked to do my own thing. I struck my first business deal as a seven-year-old, with a single packet of glow-in-the-dark stickers. My hometown is one of India's smaller cities with just over 2 million people but it is the fourth largest city in Gujarat, a state known for business people and those having a certain entrepreneurial flair. Some say business runs in our blood, and I think it just might be true.

I quickly became known around the playground as the boy with the goods: stars, horses, fairies, ducks... you name it, I had the glow-in-the-dark sticker just for you. And I made quite a tidy sum from them too. I would purchase a sheet of 20 stickers for roughly 10 rupees, and sell the stickers individually with a nice margin, of course.

My profits would then go towards satisfying my sweet tooth for shrikhand, a traditional Indian dessert made from yoghurt, flavoured with sugar, saffron and cardamom. Or I would buy sweets to soften the blow when my parents were told of my poor school grades. If I wasn't peddling stickers in the school grounds, I could be found hiding inside the bathroom at home most mornings, refusing to come out. I hated going to school, and the bathroom always felt like a safe refuge for me. Staying indoors in a classroom all day drove me nuts. I preferred being outside, playing street games and selling my goods, making a little money on my own.

My hometown has close ties to the nation's father and one of my heroes, Mahatma Gandhi. In India, we call him Gandhiji, the 'ji' being a sign of respect.

When Gandhi was a young boy, his father was the Mayor of Rajkot, and Gandhi went to school there, before he moved on to study law in London. Gandhi was never actually a great student, and neither was I. I was a naughty child always getting into trouble (most of the time it was not my fault, of course)! Summer afternoons were swelteringly hot and, as is the custom in India, my family would usually have a siesta after lunch, closing the curtains and taking a nap. Sometimes I would pretend I was sleeping and wait for my mother to fall asleep, then I would wiggle out from under her arm and disappear over our terrace wall, free like the cows, to explore the streets. I liked to visit the temple of Hanuman, a Hindu god known as the flying monkey, where I would light a candle and leave flowers.

Hanuman was to me what many sports heroes are to other kids; a role model who embodied strength, but most importantly strength of character. Hanuman was also hardworking and loyal. But nobody is perfect and he was also known to be a little reckless and naive. My loyalty and naivete are what often started many fights, verbal or physical. I had a knack for landing myself in the middle of an argument or disagreement, or I would flare up if I saw someone being mistreated or disrespected.

The best part about Hanuman though, was that he was like Superman, he was strong and could fly. Sometimes I would dream about flying - wiggling out of my mother's embrace (like I used to when sneaking out to experience real life adventures), I would get up from the mattress on which we were sleeping on the rooftop and walk to the edge. I would spread my arms and use them as wings, soaring high above the houses, food stalls and markets I knew so well from the ground. It was different up there and I remember how this dream made me feel; free and independent.

At that time, I'd heard a few stories from family friends about other places in the world, without really understanding what it meant. The concept of 'London' was my perception of everything outside India. Back then I thought it was only possible for me to experience 'London' in my dreams.

I did not take kindly to adverse comments about my family, for example if my sisters were teased, I was quick to defend them and make the bully apologise. I wouldn't let other children speak badly of, or to, their elders or teachers. Once I punched a boy in my class on the nose for being disrespectful to our teacher. Perhaps it was also my father's influence. He was always ready to protect and stand up for people.

Many times, I fought without thinking, which often meant I got into trouble, even if my heart was in the right place. I know that violence is not the answer to anything, but when I was young, I was a little hot headed, and my tendency of getting into fights, coupled with the fact that I was unable to sit still long enough to be taught much in a classroom, meant I was transferred to many different schools.

Learning in a classroom didn't excite me. I simply couldn't see the point or how I would benefit from being passive. I couldn't see how it aligned with my destination - although I had no idea where exactly I was heading at the time. No school wanted to keep a 'troublemaker' like me, and I was bored with each new school just as much as the last. I always enjoyed learning English, as most of these schools were bilingual in English and Gujarati (my mother tongue). But I valued my sense of freedom much more - I didn't want to be confined within the walls of a classroom when life was happening right outside.

I was given a bicycle as a gift for my 12th birthday, and it wasn't even second-hand, maybe fifth hand before it came to me. It was a lady's bicycle and the paint had worn off, so my grandfather and I painted it red. It wasn't pretty but it got the job done, and with this bicycle my business was really able to take off. I couldn't explain my love for business other than the rush of excitement I'd get from making a good deal, and receiving something tangible for it.

With better transport in place and some capital to invest in more things, I moved on from stickers and pens to toasted sandwich-makers and spice grinders. I'd learned how to make toasted sandwiches, a very simple meal, from one of the many sandwich-walas with roadside stalls all around the city. In Hindi 'wala' means 'one in charge'. For example, a chai-wala is a person who prepares, sells or serves tea on the side of the road or in small roadside shops. I worked with a sandwich-wala for a few weeks when the trend had rapidly spread from Mumbai to all corners of India. This delicious little meal was all the rage in the early 1990's and when I discovered the electric device that enabled these sandwiches to be made from home, I was quick to invest in a couple of them, calculate a little markup and go about selling them in my neighbourhood.

After investing most of my hard-earned money in two sandwich makers, which had cost 350 rupees each (about 10 Australian dollars), off I went, pedalling around the neighbourhood on my bicycle, knocking on doors and conducting demonstrations. Most people didn't have the money to pay the full amount, so I was smart enough to ask for a deposit and offer monthly instalments, on one condition: these buyers introduced me and my kitchen appliances to their friends.

I ended up having so many different jobs when I was a child, avoiding school in every way I could. I always liked doing something with a 'real' result, something tangible, something I could hold. I was naive back then, not understanding the wealth of knowledge that comes from education. Getting a monthly card with my grades on it just didn't seem like an achievement at all, especially when my hustling was earning me real cash in real time.

I even spent some time folding saris at a store in the market. Women would come in for one specific thing but would end up leaving with piles and piles of woven fabric, one style was always pitched as being seen on the latest Bollywood star. I was a natural salesman.

Soon I was known as the boy on the red bicycle with the good deals. Not yet a teenager, I didn't need the money but meeting new people and selling them different things was just something I liked to do and preferred to being cooped up in a classroom all day.

When I was thirteen, my mother passed away, and my father along with my brother and two sisters, moved to Mumbai. He was a big, handsome man, and a born entrepreneur. He built up a few small businesses to support his family and the community, creating employment. He sometimes helped others build businesses to support their families too, giving his time and knowledge generously. When he decided to leave town and move to the big city, he gave away these businesses to some of his friends, deciding they needed them more than he did. I saw how he just let it all go without hesitation, something I found strange at the time. Now I think he could not bear to continue life in the same place he shared with my mother and that he somehow knew none of us would be able to move on with our lives if we stayed in the same town.

Grandfather did not want to relocate, though. He was in his eighties and needed to be looked after on a daily basis. So, both he and I stayed in Rajkot together. I did not want to leave him, and to be frank, we were both quite happy and content to stay there, even though the house now felt empty and strange with just the two of us.

We were a good team; he never cared what I did outside (nor did I care what he did inside), as long as I was home to serve him 'chai' three times a day. Without my father's supervision and strict rules to adhere to, I was free to do what I pleased, and my door-to-door business boomed.

We settled into our own routine quite quickly; every morning I'd wake up, fetch Grandfather his morning tea and then head out for the day, full of plans and prospects. I would only come back in the afternoon so that we could make lunch together, then return for dinner later in the evening. We had some domestic help, and I did not have to do laundry or sweep the floors. Grandfather's only task for the day was to go to the corner shop and buy vegetables for lunch and dinner, which we would cook together.

Father had started another business in Mumbai that was going well. He would send us money, often in 10 and 50-rupee bundles, to pay for my daily expenses, covering basic needs such as food, clothes and books. I didn't need the money he sent as I was making my own, and the neat bundles of fresh, crisp notes fascinated me so much it seemed a shame to break them up and spend them. So, I would stack them up in my cupboard and watched the money accumulate slowly but steadily over time. In India, as families are usually quite large, it is rare to have your own bedroom. It is customary to have your own cupboard, though, that serves as a wardrobe and storage for all your personal items, pretty much the only private place you have in the whole house.

I always wanted to be independent, to roam about freely like the cows, forge my own path in life and make my own money. Maybe it was due to being a middle child; never getting the stature that comes with being the eldest, or the special treatment that follows from being the youngest. Either way, I was happy to be left alone and to do things my own way.

From time to time, father would visit us from Mumbai, bringing with him gifts of board games, new toys, or delicious sweets. We always had the best time, laughing and playing together. I would never get to enjoy these special games or toys for long though, because after a few hours my father would often take them from me and give them to less fortunate families down the road. I felt that Father always thought of others first, and I have to admit that I felt jealous sometimes. It was my father bringing me things and giving me attention, and I could not understand why I could not keep them, especially when he would be returning to Mumbai and leaving me behind.

Later in life he told me how he cherished the lessons he was able to teach his children more than any material object. However, it was easy to believe that he put others before his own kin and for many years I often felt neglected. In later years, I have come to really appreciate the things he taught us by bringing us up the way he did as it has made me resilient.

“There are more important things than this material life, beta,” he would say, using the Hindi word for son to somewhat soften the blow. In India, people older than you may call you ‘beta’ as a way of affection, even if not related. There was one day that I remember quite clearly - I had just got the hang of a new game involving a huge set of beautiful, shiny and colourful marbles, only to have to hand it over soon after to a girl whose family had recently lost their house. My face must have shown my unhappiness.

Father said, “These things don’t last long. You are lucky you’re not losing more than this toy - you’re lucky you were able to experience it at all - and you will have more later by letting this go. It will all come back to you.”

I begrudgingly complied, letting go of several footballs, watches and cricket bats too, wondering when 'more' would miraculously appear in front of me.

My father had always been a prominent figure in the community for as long as I could remember, with people coming to him and relying on him for advice in all kinds of matters. He now owns a large plot of land in Rajkot, that he bought in 2005. Here he has built an ashram, a retreat dedicated to the welfare of people and animals. He is helping people in our local community by giving them food, donating school supplies to young girls from nearby villages, and offering shelter to travellers. The ashram is also a favourite venue for various activities and milestone events, including weddings and other Hindu ceremonies and festivals. Throughout my childhood I saw him build several businesses, the last one given away when he decided to solely focus on the ashram, just like he'd done when leaving Rajkot for Mumbai. He let them go and passed most of them on to his employees and their families, just the same way he would do with my toys and games.

I believe that your childhood will most certainly define at least some aspects of who you are or explain why you do the things you do. Looking back, that streak of independence I had as a young boy stuck with me throughout my life - now running my own business, still giving stuff away, prioritising social impact and still having fun. A lot of that is due to my father's influence. Father, was self-made and didn't inherit wealth from his family, or from anyone else and had a giving nature above anything else. So, when he stumbled upon the mountain of rupee notes he'd sent that I'd been keeping aside in my cupboard, on one of his routine visits, he was outraged.

"I had sent you all this money and it's all here! What have you been doing to pay the bills?" He held bundles of fresh, crisp notes out in front of me, pulling them out of my wardrobe one after the other. It was then that I told him about the neighbourhood's favourite, who rode a red bicycle, and how I had built a business cycling around the neighbourhood, peddling various items. Although still upset, I like to think he was also just the tiniest bit proud of me. But he needed to set an example and he put an end to my carefree Rajkot days.

"You're coming with me to Mumbai."

I'd be leaving behind not only my beloved Grandfather but also the local cows who wandered in and out of the scenes of my childhood. I suddenly longed for their freedom, to never waver from their chosen path, even if it meant dodging traffic on their journey across busy roads. Mumbai was just one of the places serving me with opportunities as well as obstacles that I would have to navigate in this thing called life.

My Key Takeaways

- Think about how your childhood passions and upbringing shaped you into who you are today. What you liked to do as a child can help you choose a career path.
- If obstacles come your way, it's okay to adapt. You don't have to move forward in a straight line to progress in your life.
- It is important to give to others less fortunate than yourself.

Chapter 2

You Don't Need A School To Learn

"I am always ready to learn although I do not always like being taught."

– Winston Churchill

Before I moved to Mumbai, I had never had a 'nickname' but soon after arriving, I was given two: 'Fook Fook' and 'Football.'

Our rented apartment in Mumbai was not large enough for all of us to comfortably live in, and because of my unruliness, I was sent to an all-boys' boarding school in the nearby town of Nashik. It was a religious Hindu school that my father thought would instil some discipline in me. I remember standing in the school driveway when he dropped me off, with one bag in my hand and another slung over my shoulder. The yellow brick school buildings were large with big black windows, surrounded by a 2-metre-high wall. A teacher had been sent to meet me and with this stranger standing next to me I watched my father's tuk-tuk slowly disappear into the horizon, feeling abandoned and alone for the first time in my life.

"Why did he insist that I come to Mumbai if I have to live somewhere else?" I thought. I was upset and angry that he didn't even look back to wave to me.

I resented him a little bit for it, but he later told me he couldn't look back because he had been crying, torn between not wanting to leave me there and feeling that he had no other choice.

I was sixteen, which was two to three years older than most of the other boys at the boarding school. Besides the age difference, it was an English-speaking school, so I struggled from the word go. Needless to say, I had failed English in Rajkot and had little understanding of the language, even though it had been one of my favourite subjects.

Boarding school didn't exactly stop me from getting into trouble either - I somehow still got into fights and my punishments would often involve cleaning the toilets. It eventually got to the point where the wardens stopped bothering to write up a roster for toilet cleaning, it was a given that it would be me, bent down scrubbing the facilities the next morning. This was on top of the other chores I had been assigned, including cutting fruits and vegetables for lunch and dinner, as well as collecting and distributing students' mail.

It didn't take me long to conclude that I was not fit for life in a boarding school, filled with rules, schedules and restrictions. I despised being told when I could and could not sleep, when I could and could not eat and when I could and could not shit. Conformity was never my thing, I had come from Rajkot where I had lived a free and easy life with Grandfather, where even the cows were let loose from their farms to do as they pleased.

My boarding school days soon came to an end though.

The final straw occurred one day as I helped offload boxes from a truck bound for the kitchen. I stumbled across pornographic video cassettes being smuggled in, hidden under a pile of vegetables. "This is supposed to be a religious school!" I thought to myself in disbelief as I violently peeled a potato that same evening.

So, after nine months at the boarding school, I did what I thought was my only option - early one morning I packed up all my things, snuck out without telling a single soul that I was leaving and ran away. Granted, my English had improved a little, but I had failed, again!

There was a bus stop just down the road from the school and I got on the first bus that came by. One of my father's friends lived halfway between Nashik and Mumbai and had come to visit me a few times, keeping him informed about how I was doing. I decided to go to his house first, perhaps stay there for a night or two. I asked him to call my father and tell him what had happened, as I was too scared to do so myself. Father was angry at first but hearing my reasons (and they were many) he understood and was sympathetic, so he took me back to Mumbai to live with him and my siblings.

To my horror, my trusty red bicycle had been given away when I left for Nashik, and with it my independence was gone too. Mumbai traffic was much heavier than in Rajkot and Father did not allow any of his children to put themselves in danger by cycling around on the roads. I had been looking forward to riding around on my bicycle again - in my mind and dreams it had become a symbol of my freedom. I missed my squeaky but steady pedalling, all-around town with kitchen appliances hanging from the handlebars. But it was great to be reunited with my sisters and my brother again. For the first time in some years we were living like a family once more. Father had employed some domestic help, and we would get a piping hot lunch served to us every afternoon as well as supper in the evening before going to bed. My sisters were free to study, as well as my brother and I.

Being back in Mumbai didn't make me any more inclined to study, though. Quite the contrary.

My younger sister had been enrolled in a good school just around the corner from our house, and I was sent to the same school. Having skipped so many lessons and failed so many times when I was younger, I was way behind and found it difficult to fit in, especially since I was put in a class one level below my younger sister..!

Grandfather was now being looked after by a neighbouring family. His health had started to decline, but he still refused to make the move to join us all in Mumbai. He didn't like the big city and insisted on staying in Rajkot - he had heard old wives' tales of children leaving their elderly parents on the streets of Mumbai. So, I would return to visit him as often as I could and in the spirit of keeping my entrepreneurial streak alive, every time I returned, I'd bring back boxes of Rajkot's delicacy, peda: a chewy fudge-like sweet, topped with dried fruit or nuts and spiced with cardamom and saffron. I'd enlisted Father's visiting friends as my peda dealers - without them realising it - always asking for boxes of peda to top up my supply. I gave peda as gifts (otherwise known as bribes) to the teachers back in Mumbai, hoping it would result in better grades for my assignments and exams, while also selling them to my classmates, watching my passive income grow once more.

The peda business was going strong at this time but my grades - not so much.

Father continued to enrol me in extra tuition classes in the hope that my academic abilities would improve in time for the upcoming 10th standard exams, which I had already failed once. These were centralised public exams taken by students across India in Class 10 (generally when they were fifteen years old) and were essential to gain entrance to upper secondary schools. But no amount of extra maths or English tuition would ignite my interest to study, and I began to feel bad about wasting Father's money. Then I saw an advertisement for tuition classes, which said "No Pass No Fee." If I didn't pass, then at least I wouldn't waste any more money!

The tuition class was a half-hour train ride away and although I had caught trains before in Rajkot, Mumbai was a much larger city. I kept my money folded in the top pocket of my shirt and my small-town naivety got the better of me one day when I fell asleep on the train, only to wake up and find my pocket empty.

I'd had my first encounter with pickpockets and lost 500 rupees. At the time of writing this book that would be the equivalent to about 10 Australian dollars, but it was even more back then and a lot of money in Indian terms. Nerves robbed me of my appetite and my ability to speak, I was so scared Father would be angry with me after finding out I had lost the money. It was my younger sister who eventually broke the silence and told him the real reason I wasn't eating and why I'd been so quiet over dinner. I'd avoided looking up at them or speaking during the whole meal, just staring into my dal and the curry leaf floating on the top of it.

"Nilesh, it's okay that you lost the money, as long as you learnt a lesson. This is Mumbai after all, it's full of pickpockets," he said as I whimpered, head hung low.

"You are safe and that's the most important thing." He lifted my chin and offered me a peda as he looked into my teary eyes.

"I am confident that money is not lost for long anyway," he said with a twinkle in his eyes.

It wasn't until years later that I realised what he meant, that he hoped the money stolen would be put to good use, helping to put food on the table for some other family. To support that sentiment, I'd gladly have more money stolen from me, but I never put money in my shirt pocket again.

For a second time, I failed the 10th standard exam.

But I was happy knowing I had not wasted any more of Father's money on tuition. So off I skipped to collect my initial down payment.

"Hello. I failed! I'm here to take my money back," I said matter-of-factly.

"What do you mean?" the tutor asked, furrowing his brow and looking up at me from a huge stack of papers he was in the process of marking.

"No pass no fee - I didn't pass, so I don't need to pay a fee," I retorted.

The tutor smirked, realising my confusion, "You don't get that money back. You can continue to study here and receive tuition without having to pay an extra fee now that you have failed - that's what 'no pass no fee' means."

I fought hard yet left with nothing but a valuable lesson in the art of marketing spin. Now I realise that just because you put someone in a traditional classroom, it does not necessarily mean they will learn - and I was proof of that.

Parents spend so much money for education, but the student must want to be a student over everything else. My father came from a small town and being raised in a small town, we children did not spend much time on what we know as schooling today. You would be taught how to read and write, and basic mathematics but you learn practical things over theory. My grandfather was always great with his hands, fixing and making things from scratch that his family couldn't buy. My father would help him and also his mother, my grandmother. She was a community person, who did everything she could to help everyone, animals as well as people. She would give away food and clothes to the people that needed them and give shelter to animals. However, Father thought that getting an education was the right thing to do, as he wanted us to have all possible opportunities. But never once did he pressure any of us to excel in school or to be a top ranker.

Eventually, when I was nineteen, Father gave up on me ever making it through school. He was happy for me not to study, but he was firm that I did not dawdle my time away, and neither did I want to! So I was quite chuffed when he put me to work in one of his friend's computer shops; Charni Computer Services.

This was the time of the 'dot com boom' at the end of the 1990s, and my father thought that may be computers could lead to some kind of career path. The arrangement was like an internship - I didn't receive a salary, but in exchange for lifting boxes and delivering printers and computers (via crowded trains) to clients all over the city, I was given the opportunity to observe and learn. I also received half a vada pav (an Indian-style burger) every day for lunch, which I would eat while watching the hardware engineers bring computers to life by assembling memory drives, motherboards and other components. I was taught how to type, install software and how to use the internet. But creating websites piqued my interest the most.

To my own and everyone else's surprise, I decided I wanted to study web design. I found a very expensive one-year diploma course and now it was my turn to convince my family that I should study. I took the hardware engineer with me to see Father to help me pitch the merit of this course, and what great value it was. The best part was that the school didn't have any admission requirements other than paying the entry fee - they were more interested in riding the dot-com boom and, to be blunt, taking people's money.

Father agreed on two conditions; first, I needed to negotiate an instalment payment plan and secondly, I actually had to study and finish the course this time.

I agreed, and for the first time in my life, I was applying myself to learning! Everyone was excited.

The first few weeks covered the essentials from html coding, website design, user interface and Java scripting, to Photoshop, booking a domain name and using different search engines. I couldn't get enough of it - I'd found the same rush of excitement and buzz I'd felt when selling a sandwich-maker or spice grinder back in Rajkot.

I soon befriended two young men who had graduated from college and already had jobs, and were studying IT on the side - Tarun, who was highly intelligent and spoke exceptional English, and Mansoor, a talented programmer and graphic designer. Both were skinny young men with the whole world ahead of them, trying to look older than they were by wearing trousers and shirts a little too big for them, just like I did. I was even wearing glasses (without prescription) in an attempt to come across as older and wiser.

One day I shared the idea of the three of us starting a website design business together, in which we could pool our newly acquired college knowledge and our individual strengths. A sure formula to success and the first time I'd ever considered having partners in business, instead of being a lone ranger.

"It's a nice idea Nilesh, but we need investment… And, who is going to give us money?" Tarun asked pragmatically.

"We don't need investment. We just need a first project!" I said excitedly and with more than a sparkle in my eyes. "All we need is a business card and a flyer to start us off. I can find the projects, I'll do sales." We needed a name and liked the sound of 'WebMantra,' which belonged to an existing company. In Sanskrit, 'mantra' means chanting and 'tantra' means tools. We settled on WebT@ntra Web Solutions & Services.

One of Father's friends had a showroom nearby selling suitcases, so I went to see him and delivered the first WebT@ntra sales pitch, but he wasn't as willing as I'd anticipated.

"I don't need a website," he said, waving his hand dismissively.

"Well, you have all these people coming in to buy suitcases, sir, and you give them a catalogue to take away every time… Why wouldn't you just put your products online? Then you won't have to keep giving out printed photocopies which will save you money in the long run. Also, people who travel internationally and have money can see your products too!"

I was quite pleased with how I was able to come up with this on the fly, really putting all my salesman tactics to good use.

He stroked his chin in consideration, looking down at me over his spectacles.

"How much will it cost me?"

"15,000 rupees," I said, puffing out my chest.

"What - that's a lot of money!" he exclaimed.

"But sir, you will be ahead of everyone else, most importantly, your competitors!"

He told me that as his shop was very close to the international airport in Mumbai, most of his business came directly from airlines that had to fix passengers' bags damaged in transit and he didn't really need an online presence or to advertise his services. I did not give up though and he slowly came around to the idea. We booked the domain name bagrepairscentre.com. He gave me 5,000 rupees as an advance for the project.

The plan had been to continue studying and work on our new business at the same time, however, I'd never stuck at school long enough to understand the general trajectory of learning and practice, and soon I found I was becoming a bit bored with studying. Again!

I just wanted to be out in the world designing websites - and making them now - and WebT@ntra was really taking off. Spending time in a classroom didn't make sense to me and once more I had to take a risk and back myself at the consequence of disappointing my father. I could have stuck out the diploma course and made him happy, but I knew that wouldn't have made me happy.

I consulted Hanuman in my head, already knowing the option he'd choose – and I quit school for the umpteenth time.

I was already selling web design services and making money, so I stopped paying my fees, despite the fact that the course still had nine months to go in which it covered animations and hardcore programming. I continued to attend the computer labs at night for the WebT@ntra business, sneaking in with Tarun or Mansoor when they came in at night to catch up on their studies.

Sometimes, when they could not come in as they had jobs, I had to wait for the changeover of security, as the night shift guard was unaware of my non-fee-paying status. Sitting in the computer labs, we'd learn from each other and exchange ideas. I became a regular on cyberchats.com, enchanted by the idea of being able to speak with people from all over the world. But there were still a lot of English words I did not know, and I'd often ask Tarun and Mansoor to translate.

"Hey, they keep saying 'fook fook' a lot," I said one evening pointing at the chat window on my screen. Tarun and Mansoor were not there, so I turned to the person sitting next to me.

"What does 'fook' mean?"

He had a look at what I was talking about, and within seconds he bent over laughing, tears streaming down his cheeks, holding his stomach and gasping for air, realising I hadn't got the pronunciation quite right. When he was able to collect himself, he told me it was a swear word, before having another laughing fit, in which the rest of the people there joined in, including myself.

His name was Deepak and from that day on he called me Fook Fook.

It didn't take long though before I got caught for not paying tuition fees and was permanently barred from the computer labs.

We were still working on bagrepairscentre.com and solved the problem of suddenly being without our office by hiring a computer and moving our operation to a friend's apartment that had an internet connection. Within a month WebT@ntra had completed its first project and Father's friend was so happy that he gifted me a leather office satchel on top of the money.

"You're starting a new business Nilesh, and I'm your first client! This bag will help you look the part," he told me.

After deducting expenses, WebT@ntra made a profit of 7,500 rupees, which we split between the three of us. Father had found out that I'd stopped paying my fees sometime back, and one night he sat me down for a 'talk.' I was saved by the telephone as his friend called and gave a glowing review of my services. Father was happy I was at least doing something worthwhile, and while I hadn't completed my course, I had at least completed my first project.

I felt that I had finally found my purpose - a way to combine the thrill of sales with my fascination for technology and the Internet. Who knew studying and learning could further fuel my determination to succeed? Maybe this was how all the top students at my school back in Rajkot felt, I wondered. Another friend of my father's, who sold travel services, let me set up a WebT@ntra office in his shop, cementing the idea that what I was doing was 'meant to be,' with good fortune around every corner.

I purchased computer equipment on an instalment plan, but after three weeks of sitting in my new office, I wondered why I wasn't getting any business. I realised very quickly that even if you have a 'proper' office you can't just expect business to come to you. It's the same as a classroom - just because you're sitting in it doesn't mean you're going to learn something.

Nothing will just fall into your lap, not even web design projects.

With this in mind, I stuffed my leather satchel with business cards and flyers, adding magazines and newspapers to fill it out and make it look as if I had more clients. Tarun and I would target all the cyber cafés in the area. Having the Internet at home was still a novelty at this time and we thought that everyone with a business idea or start up would be at these cafés using the Internet.

Tarun and I were the perfect sales team, he'd initiate the sales pitch in English, and then I would take over in Hindi and close the deal.

"Ready to make some more deals, Fook Fook?" he said playfully before we headed out each day. He'd heard about the incident in the computer lab, as had everyone else.

We managed to get a few projects under our belt like this, but nothing lasts forever and our days of studying and playing the part of entrepreneurs came to an end pretty quickly.

Soon Tarun left for the United States and Mansoor found a job in the Middle East.

I'd become a lone ranger once more and continued to build up a client list and run WebT@ntra by myself. This was a time before mobile phones were common, and I'd managed to earn enough from my work to purchase myself a pager. It can be very easy to get caught up or absorbed in your bubble of passion and purpose.

I learnt early on the importance of not letting work rule your life. Distracted by deadlines and chasing new clients on one unusually busy day, I missed my pager buzzing incessantly in my pocket. Or maybe subconsciously I'd blocked it out, for nothing else but work and my business mattered in that moment. My sister and brother were trying to contact me to let me know Grandfather had passed away. I never got to say a proper goodbye. The grief was enough to instil in me the importance of regularly checking in with family, and I never have my phone on silent mode even today.

At this point, my father walked away from another business and workshop he had built after arriving in Mumbai and handed it over to a family he deemed needed it more. I'd seen him doing this quite a few times, and I know it has made an impact on who I am as well.

It taught me that nothing lasts forever and that's ok. In essence it's karma, what goes around comes around.

Father had once more become a centre point in the community, just as he had been in Rajkot. He always was community oriented, helpful, social and loved by many. During this time, he became more serious about his role as a public servant and my older sister had decided to follow him on that path, too. He let go of his business to be able to submerge himself totally in his cause of animal and human welfare, just like his mother had done before him. But not before seeing that his children were secure, with a proper place to live and setting them up with opportunities for a good income for years to come. He, like many Gujaratis, had a real talent for business. What put him a notch above others, was his aptitude for mediation and negotiation. Mumbai was a growing city, and the real estate market was on the cusp of a boom. My father not only secured a few properties or patches of land to sell 10 or 20 years later, he did the same for many others. Making sure that people would get the best deals and not be taken for a ride by the real estate developers. He bought an apartment big enough for all of us to live in, in Juhu, a very good suburb in Mumbai, famous for its beach and celebrities.

Due to Father's outgoing and friendly nature, and his problem-solving abilities he made many friends and gained even more followers.

Maneck and Phiroze Patel were a middle-aged married couple from the Parsi community who had become close friends, not only with my father, but they also took a liking to his children. Inherently so, we addressed them as Aunty and Uncle. In India, we call anyone older than us 'aunty' or 'uncle'. It is a sign of respect, just like touching the feet of an elder.

The two of them looked quite impressive; Uncle with his dashing suits, elegant moustache and booming voice, and Aunty with a modern short haircut and exquisite silk sarees. They did not have children of their own as they had found each other and married later in life. So they both took to me as if I was their own son. They were both very successful individuals and made a huge impact on my life, becoming my adopted principals in a way. They saw how well I was doing but thought my broken English was holding me back from reaching my true potential.

One of my fondest memories of them is of my introduction to western cutlery. I'd grown up accustomed to the Indian way of eating with one's hands. Like Ariel in the Little Mermaid, a fork could have been a hair comb for all I knew.

As members of the very exclusive Cricket Club of India (CCI), Aunty and Uncle treated me to many western meals. I would tuck into a plate of pasta, trying not to stab myself in the face with my knife and fork, newly learnt concepts to me. Learning the western ways of life and etiquette helped me immensely when I eventually travelled the world. They taught me so much and brought stability to my life, but most importantly taught me the value of education - despite all resistance and non-interest on my part.

Maneck Aunty was a French professor at Jai Hind College, one of Mumbai's most esteemed colleges, and in her youth, she had spent a year in France as an exchange student. She believed that "education is everything" and insisted I go back to school. But I couldn't see how it aligned with my purpose and where I wanted to go in life - I already had a business, I was making money, and I was getting by just fine without improving my English skills, so why would I go back to school?

With WebT@ntra flourishing and my confidence as a businessman growing, my sights were set on Cipla, one of Asia's largest pharmaceutical companies. They were looking for a website design consultant on a short-term contract, and I could only imagine the extra traction I would get with a name like Cipla listed as one of WebT@ntra's clients.

I arrived at Cipla's reception to see thirty other applicants dressed in suits and ties, carrying three-page resumes, and every single one of them at least five years senior to my twenty. Meanwhile, I was dressed in shirt and trousers, no blazer or suit jacket and with experience that barely filled half a page; I was a secondary school dropout, with a list of recent websites I had designed along with some hobbies.

The interviewers offered to speak in Hindi, but I insisted on continuing the interview in English. "My Aunty says if I not practice English, I not learn," I said, stumbling over the words as I went but still making myself understood.

They looked at each other and must have thought, "What are you thinking young man, this is not the time to be practising your English... in a job interview..."!

"Okay, you want English, we'll speak in English, no problem."

I was mixing up English with Hindi and vice versa but somehow, they understood my answers in relation to colour schemes, hierarchy in website design, layouts, and html. After leaving I thought nothing more of it - I didn't stand a chance against those other professional-looking candidates. But a week later I was back at Cipla's reception, for my second interview and this time

I dressed for the part. I felt incredibly smart wearing a blue suit, with a gold Cross pen, Phiroze Uncle had given me, resting in my top pocket. I still carry the same pen with me every day. It reminds me of him and his blessings and, on more than one occasion, I have felt my heart jump in fear of having lost it. I hope I never do! I touched my pen for luck in getting through to the next round - finalists were given two weeks to develop concept designs for their main website and a secondary doctor-facing site. I worked hard on it for the next two weeks and I submitted my concept via post: a printed brochure, on a CD, a website address, and a floppy disk (for the younger generation, it was the early 2000s version of a USB thumb drive), just to be sure.

A tip for students, job seekers and those about to give an important business presentation: never trust one method to work. Isn't it the worst when your PowerPoint presentation will not open, or the sound is missing, or you find you have saved the wrong file? Always keep extra copies, just in case!

As for Cipla, I got the job.

It turned out that despite not passing out of high school or having a degree I was among the few who had practical work experience. Later, I also wondered if they had chosen me as I was also likely the naivest of all other applicants, knowing they could take me for a ride by lowballing fees.

They told me I'd be developing concepts, but the actual web designing work would be contracted to another company. I'd never priced for consultancy work before and when they asked what I would charge I told them I didn't know. I was more focused on seeing the look on the faces of my aunty and uncle when I told them the good news.

"Uncle! Aunty! I got the job, and they are paying me 3,800 rupees a month!" I happily exclaimed, rushing through the door of their house. I was spending almost all of my free time with them. Maneck Aunty really understood me and what made me tick, she could see I had potential and never for a second wanted to give up on me.

"Nilesh, no!" she threw her arms in the air, upset.

"Do you know the security guard in this building is probably getting ten times more money than that! It's one of the largest pharmaceutical companies in the world!"

She quickly turned to her husband; "I told you to go with him!"

"Aunty, don't worry about the money; think of all the people I beat for the job!" I tried to reason.

"Yes, you passed the interview, very well done but you don't know how to charge for your services, beta."

A week or so later, when I had started the job, I approached the two Cipla interviewers, who were now my project managers and tried to put on my best serious expression.

"My Aunty tells me I'm not charging you enough," I said, wagging my finger.

"No, you are not," they chuckled.

"Well, I want one thing from you. I want you to write me a reference letter for this work," I said, folding my arms.

"But you're not working here, you're consulting, we can't do that," they said, shaking their heads.

"It's only fair, I want that letter" I said.

That was the beginning of the 'Great Letter Feud' that would last until I completed my design work. Relentless persistence wore them down and I finally got my way - I just needed to ask, ask and ask again to get that letter of recommendation with the official Cipla stamp. I had got so caught up in 'winning' and impressing my family that I completely undervalued myself - an easy target for being taken advantage of in the business world.

That reference letter was more than just a reference letter - it was a reminder that had I stood up for myself, and also a certificate of valuation, tangible proof that I was valuable, and little did I know just how handy it would be in the years to come... It is so important for any student, migrant or budding entrepreneur to keep their documents organised and accounted for.

In 2002, the dot-com bubble burst and the whole website industry crashed. In the prior years, the massive growth of Internet-related industries caused stock markets to rise, largely based on speculation, that soon caused stocks to nosedive, and the Internet services world itself to become heavily oversupplied.

Thousands of people were now offering website design services and shops had started to put boards outside: Please, no dotcom services. I felt that my life purpose was being derailed - I was like the cow in Rajkot, standing in the middle of peak hour traffic, competitors zooming all around me. But I didn't have as much luck as India's sacred cow in surviving - I felt that any minute my business and I would join the flies and other insects on the windscreen of the next truck, or in my case, the next business to turn me away.

Maneck Aunty was quick to swoop in with her endless reasons of why I should finish school and enrolled me in the National Institute of Open Schooling in Delhi, conducted via distance learning, which meant I could study from home.

Whether it was the relaxed feeling of a home environment, the fact that I now had more life experience under my belt, or the fact that the open school allowed me to select my own subjects and give up maths and science, I finally passed the 10th standard.

I hadn't realised just how much my English had improved from working with those online cyberchat.com groups, and listening to audio tapes Maneck Aunty and Phiroze Uncle had, which helped me to improve my language skills.

My English was far from perfect, but something had clicked inside me - school was no longer too difficult to understand, but a challenge I could overcome if I set my mind to it. Passing subjects without too much grief, I now wanted to go all the way and finish those last years of high school. I could finally see the value in education, and I was starting to realise how it aligned with my purpose.

My family, Aunty and Uncle were very pleased with my achievements and one day when we were all having lunch together in our Juhu apartment Phiroze Uncle said; "Nilesh, you are like a football!

You get kicked around everywhere but no matter where you get kicked, you always end up getting a goal!"

"No," Father chimed in. "He is exactly like a football, bouncing from one thing to another, unable to fully commit, finish anything that he started or indeed score a goal but still playing in the game of life!"

My brother started laughing, and soon we all were roaring with laughter. They were both right, in a way - I did jump around a lot.

Maneck Aunty and Phiroze Uncle really believed in me though and told me they would support me every step of the way. So, at the age of twenty-three, and intent on proving him wrong, I told my father, "I'm going to finish high school."

The very next day in a moment of blissful synchronicity that's usually reserved for movie screens, I found my answer while skimming through the pages of The Times of India newspaper. I'd never forgotten my dreams of flying and going to this foreign place, Father's friends called London. My eyes widened as they moved from left to right over the map of England, the Tower of London and the words "Cambridge International Standard A Levels" printed underneath the logo for RIMS International School, located in an upmarket neighbourhood in Juhu, just a ten minute walk from my home.

"Aunty, I'm going to London," I proclaimed, pushing the newspaper across the table to her. Perhaps there was something to this whole education thing after all.

My Key Takeaways

- You don't need to sit within four walls and a roof to learn or be a student: sometimes, the best lessons are taught outside of school. Real world experience is invaluable, but formal education is something that is needed and valued in today's world.
- Make time for family in between studying and working. Time on this earth is precious and limited, just like my grandfather's life. Find a good phone plan if you're abroad or set up regular calls via the internet with your loved ones back home.
- Know your value and your worth: do your research and price your services based on facts, rather than excitement!

- Collect reference letters, acknowledgements, testimonials and diplomas as you go and keep them safe. They will come in handy at some stage in your life, either when applying to university, getting a job or for visa applications.
- Don't be afraid of aiming high and going for an interview above your level. Worst case scenario - you learn something new and you're more experienced when you go for another job interview. Don't stress about it, just go in and have some fun!
- To start a business, you need your first client, contrary to popular belief where there's a strong focus on securing investors before you start to offer your products or services, I believe in creating and adjusting as you go. Working with your first client and their requirements will teach you everything you need to know, but you need to treat the client right and deliver on your promises. The first client's testimonial will lead to your second one.

Chapter 3

You're Never Too Old To Get An Education

"Formal education will make you a living; self-education will make you a fortune."
— Jim Rohn

I had finally found my 'ticket' to getting out to see the world, but I would have to experience a fair amount of turbulence before I was able to land on my feet. My dream was to go to London and my first challenge was gaining admission to RIMS International School and Junior College.

Newly opened and very promising, RIMS was also a convenient choice as my father had already invested in two properties in Juhu that were close to the school. I reasoned with him that RIMS was the perfect place to continue my education. I already had a place to stay and wouldn't have to go through the ordeal of boarding school and sharing - or worse, cleaning toilets like I had before in Nashik.

After seeing the advertisement in the newspaper, I started to notice posters all over Mumbai with the slogan 'Freeing minds to achieve excellence' and promises of producing the 'best of the best' students under Britain's Cambridge International Education standard. The advertisements and posters had pictures of the Tower of London, a place I saw as a true symbol of success. I also learnt that while the school was fairly new, it had become known for teaching youth from wealthy families or those whose parents were in Bollywood. I had to attend this school!

Interviews, entrance exams and a track record of high school grades were customary to secure a place at RIMS, so I knew it was going to take a lot more than a box or two of peda to sweeten the deal this time. I needed to think bigger. In addition, obtaining school admission in India is incredibly difficult - even corrupt methods are used. Sometimes, it's not as simple as taking tests, getting good grades, or submitting a unique project to be selected to gain entry. There are many situations where large amounts of money are exchanged 'under the table' or where budding students must be creative. Rajkumar Hirani's Bollywood film '3 Idiots' illustrates this quite well, where one boy buys a uniform and simply walks into the school undetected. But for a school like RIMS, I had to be more innovative than that, especially considering I already had the whole system stacked against me, backed by a track record of poor grades and multiple exam failures... I needed to think radically and perhaps put some of my morals aside in favour of thinking of the 'big picture'.

My father, older sister and I arrived at the beachside location for the first stage of the application process: a meeting with the principal. It was the way they were dressed - like stereotypical community workers with loose fitting white tunics or kurtas down to their ankles and baggy pants - that would play an important part in my 'getting into RIMS mission'.

As expected, the first thing the principal asked was to see my previous education records. Although I had failed the 10th standard many times, I was far from stupid and realised that highlighting my lack of academic achievement was probably not a great idea. I eagerly pushed the recently received National Institute of Open Schooling in Delhi 10th standard certificate across the table to him, showing I had passed it with flying colours.

"This looks good, but where are all your other records?" he asked, sensing that he might be wasting time on someone who had flunked the interview before it even took place.

Hanuman likely shook his head at me that day considering what I was about to say, and with good reason, too. Even to this day I can't believe the words that tumbled out of my mouth; "I lost everything in the earthquake sir," I said, eyes downcast as I invented my new reality.

There had been a terrible earthquake in Gujarat a few years prior and the natural disaster had caught national attention, with scenes of destroyed homes and ruined livelihoods flashed all over television screens and plastered on the front pages of every newspaper.

"Oh, I see... what a sad story, I'm so sorry you lost everything," his voice softened a bit, and he looked over to my father and sister. "And what about your parents? Siblings or other family members?"

"Oh yes, well I lost them too. Nothing was left but me, sir," I said. "All gone, family and documents."

I felt my father and sister shift uncomfortably in their chairs and I could hear my sister's thoughts screaming, head nodding furiously; Father, what on earth is he up to! We're sitting right here, and he's gone and killed us in front of this principal!

My father sat still in his chair; hands folded in his lap and kept his calm as always, not even a small twitch to show any reaction he might have had. He was seemingly just waiting for me to carry on, possibly figuring out a suitable punishment for what I was doing, shocked to his core.

"These kind people," I continued, pointing to my father and sister, "have an ashram working for human and animal welfare. I am an orphan and they are looking after me, and have offered to pay the fees for my education. I'm very sorry that I don't have any paperwork or certificates that I can show you, but I lost everything," I said, gesturing towards my family members, who were in utter disbelief of the situation I had put them in.

"Sir, these people are a blessing, they have truly been a saviour for me."

The principal looked at me with soft eyes.

"Young man, we don't usually get students like this," he paused, lost in thought.

"We typically need the required education records but, on this occasion, I am sure we can make an exception. However, there will still be fees you will need to pay."

My father and sister did not know much about A Levels or the Cambridge International Examination Standard at this point, nor the real reason why I was so set on attending this expensive school - they were just excited that as a young man in his early twenties, I finally had an interest in finishing my studies.

"That is okay, we will cover the cost for him," my father said much to my surprise. I was amazed at how he played along, raising his palms like some kind of deity.

"But we will need an instalment scheme and a discount for the social service we are doing for him."

Minutes after that conversation, I felt really bad, as I realised how I had just used tragedy to advance my position in the world.

While I'm still not proud of those actions, as you will understand by the end of this chapter, I didn't let that opportunity go to waste.

I am certain the principal had seen through my little act, but he still gave us a discount, a payment plan and better yet, I was somehow granted exemption from those entrance exams and additional interviews.

I had done it!

I received a long lecture from my father on the right and wrong ways to achieve my desires and goals in life, but he was not too hard on me. I think he realised that this was my chance to really do something, and to overcome my previous struggles with studies. To be something different and to make something of myself, without having the education records and good results most people would have by now.

First stop RIMS, next stop London!

However, there was plenty more turbulence to come. Returning to school at the age of twenty-four, significantly older than my peers, brought with it a whole range of challenges. I was an outsider from the beginning: a young man and not a boy still in his puberty, who spoke broken English with a very heavy accent, dressed like a professor with my lucky leather bag slung over my shoulder.

Gossip began to circulate in the building's corridors, confirmed by fleeting glances and hushed whispers, discussing how it was even possible for someone like me to get into RIMS. I didn't fit in. But that was okay. I had found a place of solace in the school library - and had befriended the school librarian, Professor Edwin Canvin.

He was a kind and refined British man whose blue eyes would crinkle when he smiled, something he did a lot.

Edwin used to be a professor in his home country and was now in India to attract students to study in the UK. He looked after the library, but it was more like an office with floor to ceiling bookshelves covering all four walls and just enough of a gap to fit a door. The books were immaculately organised and pulled out to the edge of the shelf. I liked being in there. The smell of books, old newspapers and his cologne was somehow very comforting, I felt at ease.

Edwin took it upon himself to improve my English further and set me the task of reading the entire Times of India before 8 am every morning. The newspaper was written in English, and from 8.30 to 9 am every morning (including weekends, no skimping here) he sat with me in the library, at his desk in the middle of the room, before classes began. Both of us held our own copy of the huge paper, covering the desk entirely. Phiroze Uncle wasn't happy that I stole his newspaper every day, but he must have known it was for a good reason and he never complained.

Edwin would randomly choose a page and quiz me on the headlines to test me and make sure I understood what I was reading.

I spent many of my lunch hours with Edwin too, hungry for more details of his home country and stories of London, and because I'd always been better at getting along with people who were older than me.

The days of passing subjects rather easily in the Delhi National Open School were behind me and I found myself failing most of my classes again. It wasn't out of the carelessness or lack of interest, which had prevented me from advancing in my younger years -

this time it was a genuine struggle to keep up with high grading standards and cultural differences.

I was stumped for weeks over the sudden introduction of more academic terms, particularly words related to accounting, one of the subjects I was interested in but found too similar to mathematics, the very subject I had skipped to pass my 10th standard. 'Subtraction' was a foreign word in the beginning, but I soon realised it was just another way of saying 'minus'.

Then there was the challenge of learning western currency signs. Naturally, students and teachers alike were confused and slightly alarmed; "This young man doesn't know anything... who on earth let him in, what is he doing in this classroom?"

I befriended Roop around this time - he was a smart young man and exceptional at English, and he knew western currencies. We got talking after the class one day after he'd taught me the difference between £ and €.

Other subjects were English, economics, computing, and business studies and I was struggling in all of them.

After a few weeks, with the weight of constant failure on my shoulders, I asked to see the principal.

"Sir, I don't understand any of this," I tried to hold back tears but the floodgates had already burst.

"I'm finding it so hard, but I really want to learn. I don't want to give up, I need extra help," I sobbed into my hands covering my face.

The principal had developed a soft spot for me, but whether he truly believed my orphan story or not, I never found out. Teachers were instructed to give me some extra time after school hours and as they had witnessed my perseverance in the classroom, they agreed to help me.

My teachers warmed up to me after spending so much time with me. I was not surprised that my name was put forward for class president when the annual student union elections arrived. I was up against two other boys, who were very popular and wealthy, as well as a girl who had a car. She would drive the other students to McDonalds, buying them fries and milkshakes to win their vote.

I didn't have much money, but what I did have was design skills, developed during my time creating websites, putting me ahead of the competition when it came to creating our campaign posters. I took inspiration from a popular Bollywood movie at the time, Main Hoon Na (which means "I am here") featuring Bollywood star Shah Rukh Khan. In the movie, he went undercover as an older student, so it was quite fitting in many ways. Using one of the movie posters with his silhouette on a bridge, as a template, I fired up my Photoshop 5.5 and added a 24/7 clock, the RIMS logo and my name, and wrote: If you need any support, Main Hoon Na, I'm here for you.

The poster became very popular throughout the school and to my surprise, I received some votes, though not quite enough to compete with free rides to the golden arches.

Nevertheless, the teachers and students' union decided to select both of us to represent the class on the committee. However, within a few weeks, when we needed to contribute ideas at meetings, my fellow class representative dropped out. The short-lived popularity contest was over, and it seemed no number of fries could make up for the real work that had begun! I did my best to perform my elected duties. I think I did a pretty good job, but I never stood for an election again. Some personalities mesh well with politics; some people thrive under that dynamic. Not me. I couldn't quite put my finger on it at the time, but there was something unfulfilling about change from the top-down. It's change from the ground up - volunteering, kindness - that really makes a difference.

I spent many evenings with my new friend Roop. He'd tutor me in English in return for me covering for him, promising his mum he wasn't playing video games, whenever she'd call to check on us.

Just when it seemed I was really starting to gain some acceptance from my peers, turbulence hit again. I had gotten wind of a play that was to be staged at an upcoming student union end of year celebration night, where I was to be the unwitting main character.

One afternoon, Roop told me that a few students had started rehearsing a skit that poked fun at me, my weird sense of style, funny accent, and my poor English. They planned to present it on stage in front of the entire school. I asked to see the principal again, this time my eyes glassy from anger.

"Nilesh, you shouldn't be upset," he said, waving his hand dismissively.

"Sir, they're making fun of me!" I protested.

"Actually, they are doing this because they like you," the principal said.

"You are a person who cannot be forgotten easily and it's a good thing they're making fun of you. Your differences will make you famous and it means people will remember you. So don't worry."

"But it's not right, sir!" I retorted.

"It's not good because I don't feel happy about them making fun of me and everyone in the whole school will laugh at me."

My anger had subsided. My desire for acceptance was greater than my rage but I was still feeling upset about the pending humiliation.

"Well, Nilesh, why don't you laugh back at them, then?" the principal said. "Improve your English and pass your English exam. Look past the joke and take this as a challenge to truly improve your English. Stay out of trouble and fights, focus on your studies instead."

The students took to the stage, and I sat there numb, staring blankly ahead as everyone made fun of me, pointing and laughing. I had been the brunt of the joke for too long and I was determined to prove everyone wrong.

For the next few months, I kept largely to myself and studied almost every hour of every day. I kept some of my business activities going while studying at RIMS. I found a Japanese logo design book at a roadside book shop that inspired me to create my own company logos and business cards, on the side.

But my main focus was passing my A Levels.

I continued my Times of India reading sessions with Edwin in the library every morning. After my school sessions with teachers every evening, I'd head to Shiv Sagar on Juhu beach, one of Mumbai's most popular restaurants, to continue studying. The change of environment did me good and I would occupy a table for four in the corner all by myself, hunkering down and concentrating again. The manager didn't mind. I'd known him for a few months, and he knew what I was doing and saw how hard I was working.

Sometimes he would even reserve my spot and offer me a free glass of watermelon juice.

After studying at Shiv Sagar, I'd head to my extra English tuition classes and later, when the final exams were just around the corner, Maneck Aunty found me an accountant who would sit with me from 10 pm to midnight. Together we solved five years' of Cambridge accounting exams over six months. Every time there was a test, I would cry, but Maneck Aunty relentlessly continued to support and encourage me, chipping in with fees for the extra tuition every now and then.

I wanted to give up many times, and probably would have if she had stopped supporting me.

"You can do it, have faith, don't worry you will pass, beta. You'll be fine. Now, let us go and bring today's newspaper to uncle."

Phiroze Uncle had been in and out of the hospital for a few months, his health deteriorating quickly. I would go and see him as often as I could, sometimes bringing the Times of India to him after my reading sessions with Edwin. Aunty and I would sit next to his bed and discuss the news. He also encouraged and supported me to keep going, and to never lose faith in myself.

It's exactly what I needed to keep going - having someone believe in you, when you don't believe in yourself is extremely powerful.

The days blurred into weeks and before I knew it the end of the school year was approaching. "What do you want to do next Nilesh, once you pass your A Levels?" Edwin asked one day over lunch in the small library.

"I want to fly. It's my childhood dream," I said promptly without thinking. You may remember how I often dreamt I was flying, using my arms as wings and soaring high above the Rajkot rooftops. "I have always wanted to fly, and I want to go to London."

"Why London?" Edwin enquired inquisitively, he folded his hands on the desk in front of him and leant towards me a little.

I'd developed a fascination for that mystical land for as long as I could remember. I treasured stories I had heard from the many friends and family members who visited us and brought English chocolates and biscuits and tales of funny looking double-decker buses and constant rain. I told him this.

"I made a promise to myself to go there one day," I continued. "Although I never really knew how. I knew it would be hard to get a visitor's visa and permanent residency was pretty much impossible, so I realised the easiest entry was to go there as a student. But now I have a desire to study, and I want to do an undergraduate degree. I really feel in my gut that this is the right path for me."

Edwin quickly gathered a list of university websites for me to explore and encouraged me to shortlist some courses. It was a little left field given my history with computers, but I settled on a BA in Airline and Airport Management; a course that had just been introduced at Thames Valley University (now known as the University of West London.)

"This is a big decision, Nilesh, this will form your life's work, your career," Edwin said, a little perplexed by my choice.

Once more I let my mind wander back to those rooftop sleep-outs in Rajkot, where I would float over the city's temples and streets.

"I have always wanted to see the world and travel," I explained, "This industry will give me a chance. I had already looked into becoming a steward for an airline. I know I don't exactly have the looks and having to serve alcohol and meat to people goes against my principles. I can't become a pilot; my maths isn't strong enough. But I want to do this course, really, I do."

"It sure is an unusual choice," he raised his eyebrows and smiled; "But fine, if it's what you really want, you should do it."

I thought back to the cows in Rajkot, was this really my purpose? I was sure even those determined cows changed their destination every now and then, or were distracted by other desires along the way, like fresh grass. I applied for a student visa and Father agreed to support me to go to the UK.

By this time, my dearest Phiroze Uncle had passed away, but Maneck Aunty continued to help me to get ready to chase my dream.

One evening after dinner she called me into her room. She unlocked her cupboard and took out a small, royal blue, velvet bag and asked me to come and sit next to her on the bed for a minute. She handed me the little bag.

"Uncle asked me to give this to you," she said.

I opened the small knot, being careful not to break the delicate strings. I knew what it was even before I took it out onto my hand. It was his ring.

When they got married, they had a matching set of jewellery made. A pendant for her and a ring for him, made from the same cut of ruby, emerald and sapphire. To this day the ring is the only piece of jewellery I ever wear, apart from my wedding ring. I remember him by looking at it every day.

The RIMS A Level exams were graded in Cambridge and delivered back to India via post. When they arrived all the teachers met before the official announcement was given to review the results. Just after the meeting, I felt my new Nokia mobile phone buzz in my pocket - it was a text from the teacher who taught me computer studies, "Good for you Nilesh, great work!"

So, I had some hope that I had passed at least one subject.

Two days later my classmates and I sat nervously in an assembly to learn how we had performed. I tried to embody Hanuman's strength and touched my uncle's ring for luck. The principal walked onto the stage. I closed my eyes and took a deep breath.

"Before I announce these results, I want to start by congratulating Nilesh Makwana," he said.

My name echoed in the hall; everyone was silent.

"He reminded me today that "where there is a will, there is a way" and I'm pleased to say that he has passed all his subjects, most importantly English!"

With every eye in the room turned towards me, I sat there dumbfounded. The jeers and pointing fingers of my peers a few months prior were now replaced by thunderous applause and whooping congratulations.

The principal had taught me a valuable lesson; no one was going to step in and fight your battles for you in the real world, but if you held your head high and strived to do the right thing, somehow things could work out okay.

More importantly, I realised that a strong and silent approach to victory could be so much more satisfying than if I had reverted to my old ways and thrown a punch or two their way. I'd substituted brains for fists, and I had come out on top.

The next week, I made the front page of the school newsletter: "Where there is a will, there is a way" the headline read, "in celebration of Nilesh Makwana, an example of a student who pursued his dreams relentlessly."

My hard work had paid off and I had never seen Father or Maneck Aunty so happy and proud as on this day or the day I received my acceptance letter from the University of West London. Boarding that plane for London was no longer a fantasy. I felt like a true champion going in the right direction. I had support from my family, I was making money through my business, and I was having a great time with my friends driving around the city in my first car, which Phiroze Uncle had given to me, a small white Fiat.

After finishing my A-Levels at RIMS, I had picked WebT@ntra up again. I was buzzing around town in my new car, delivering projects and having meetings. I felt like a proper businessman. One day a group of young men came in to one of the cyber cafés I was using as my office to manage my web design projects. It was close to the Hare Krishna temple in Juhu and they were on a school trip, visiting from Punjab.

We quickly became close friends and I took them under my wing while they were in my city, taking them around, and showing them all the good spots in Mumbai. Later, I went to visit them in Punjab in north India. This was the first time in my life that I put on some real weight. The food they kept feeding me was just too good.

One of the young men, Shakti, and I became very close, and he applied for a visa to the UK at the same time as I did. Both of us ran around together, collecting all the documents we needed for the visa application - including bank statements, new passport photos, proof of financial support and photocopies of our offer letters from the university. We had high hopes and dreams for the next chapter of our lives.

The world was at our feet, ready to be conquered. Then our UK visas were rejected!

My Key Takeaways

- Don't let social constraints come in the way of your goals: whether it is your age, background or education level. Let your work and determination speak for itself.
- Getting into school politics and standing for class president elections can be a lot of fun but be aware that it can get messy, and you may lose friends over it too.
- It is important to have people that believe in you. Our family members, especially the older ones, can be a great source of knowledge and wisdom. Surround yourself with seniors willing to help you.
- There's no secret to success but hard work. I was motivated to go to London and education was only a step on the ladder for me to achieve this.
- People are willing to help those who want to help themselves.

Chapter 4

How To Leave Everything You've Ever Known

"Accept hardship as a necessary discipline."
– Lailah Gifty Akita

I wasn't going to let a visa rejection get in the way of pursuing my dreams. I sprang into action, organised letters from RIMS teachers and the principal. I asked them to write why I should be given the opportunity to study abroad. Not only that, but why an Indian youth - who had never been in an aeroplane, let alone left the country - should be given the chance to study aviation.

The odds were stacked against me, right?

I shook off those odds and told them: "I'm going to London. Period."

Perhaps that experience made all the difference; sometimes it's the best things in life that take the most work or follow a series of rejections, or pain.

When my second visa application came back with the stamp of approval, I appreciated it even more. Shakti on the other hand did not pursue his UK visa. He got an Australian student visa instead.

I was very excited for him, and my family was extremely excited for me.

"Nilesh really is going to London," my youngest sister squealed in excitement. Tears started to well up in her eyes and she flung her arms around my neck. I don't think I quite realised what I was about to do, leave everyone behind and pursue my own happiness. I had three weeks to get my affairs in order, and to say goodbye to everyone before I left. Most of the time people were excited and proud of what I had achieved, but there were some sad moments, too.

Maneck Aunty and my sister gathered supplies, clothes, toiletries, snacks and much more to help me set up my life in London. Father organised celebrations and Hindu rituals to see me off in a proper way. Surrounded by family and friends, I was the proudest I had ever been in my life - I'd finally applied myself to school and look at what I had accomplished, against all odds!

With my family fussing over every single item I would need to move abroad, I arrived at Mumbai Airport's international terminal for the first time in my life. I was wearing pants with pockets running down the length of my leg and two jackets in which to stuff the extra items that wouldn't fit in my luggage, which already weighed almost triple the allowance.

Thankfully, because I had previously designed the bagrepairscentre.com website, the owner pulled a few strings using his contacts at the airport, and I did not have to pay anything extra for the bags. I watched my suitcases disappear along the conveyor belt feeling exhilarated and eager to get going. But I had a knot in my stomach. Now was the time to say goodbye to my family. It was a tearful affair, but also full of blessings and love. I put my backpack on my shoulders and walked towards security.

This was it, the big moment you see in the movies, I turned to wave at my family one last time and off I went through the security gates. Then, after a short wait, I stepped onto an aircraft for the first time in my life.

During take-off, I felt uneasy. To calm myself I repeated a sacred Indian chant - the Gayatri mantra - over and over in my head, keeping my eyes firmly shut, gripping the armrests with both hands. When the wheels left the tarmac, I felt I had left my stomach back in India.

I prayed to Hanuman and wondered how he could possibly enjoy flying so much. My stomach continued to do a backflip as the plane climbed higher in the sky. But my worries soon melted away when I opened my eyes to peek through the little window, mesmerised by the sights below.

Just as in my childhood dreams I was flying high above buildings - except now I was in the clouds for real, and little did I know, this would be the first of hundreds of flights to come.

Before I arrived in London, I couldn't even point out the UK on a map. My family used to joke that London is everything that's not India. There was no 'international' it was just London. Many Indians migrated in the 1950s and 1960s, and you can still hear people in India saying that his or her family member moved to London, while it actually is Belgium or Canada. For many, London is not a place, it's a concept.

Geography was, as with most other subjects in school, not my strong suit. Yet here I was, walking through the airport gates leading me to Terminal 4 at Heathrow Airport. At the time, I did not realise how this very place would shape my life, just a year from now.

Having all the necessary paperwork clutched in my hand, I resolutely walked towards the immigration desk and security.

The first thing that struck me was that there were hardly any white people around. Lots of the staff were Indian and for a split second I wondered if I'd missed my stop, like you do on a train when you doze off. For a second I thought I had arrived back in Mumbai!

I had imagined myself as being the only person with brown skin and black hair at the terminal, but there were so many people in every shade possible. Even the man that called me to the immigration desk was Indian. In addition to not being able to point out London on a map, my knowledge of the British Empire, its colonial history and emigration of Indians to all corners of the world was almost non-existent!

The immigration officer went through my paperwork and grilled me with a series of questions that I tried my best to answer in my haze of exhaustion.

Blinking back the beckoning call of sleep, I scanned the area outside the immigration hall, taking it all in. It was the first time I had seen so many foreigners in one place, a burst of cultures and ethnicities. And not a single sign written in Hindi anywhere, they were all in English, and I found I had to read each sign carefully and not just give them a glance like you would if they were in your native language.

Soon after picking up my luggage at the carousel, I noticed a young Japanese man holding a piece of paper with my name on it. When you sign up to study abroad, the universities usually offer to organise someone to meet you at the airport and guide you to your pre-planned place to stay. I felt relieved that someone was waiting for me, even though I didn't know him.

"Welcome to London! I'm Susuma Hara, I am from the international student's office," he said, beaming at me. A split second later, his eyes widened in disbelief when he saw the vast amount of my luggage. My trolley loaded with bulging suitcases received a lot of judgemental looks from people passing by, but what I saw on his face was pure dread. Susuma had been instructed to take me to a YMCA located near the campus via London's underground, but seeing my suitcases, all of them nearly bursting at the seams, he instantly realised there was no way we were going to navigate London's labyrinth of tunnels and escalators.

"Lots of...bags..." he said trying to lift one, his attempt at small talk falling as flat as he nearly did, trying to haul the weight. He looked concerned.

"I only have enough money for the tube..." his voice trailed off, as he was lost in thought trying to figure out how he could rectify the situation.

"It's okay, I have money. I can pay for both of us," I said as I looked outside and saw a traditional London cab for the first time. It looked just like those depicted on the biscuit tins Father's friends would give us. It was late in the evening now and when the doors slid open and I stepped out of the airport I was immediately startled by the cold February air.

I had read many stories about snow, rain and winter, but I'd never truly experienced cold weather.

Wise from her days in France, Aunty had insisted that I brought a pair of gloves, I gratefully put them on. It felt a bit weird to have clothing on my hands, and I opened and closed my hands a couple of times to get used to the feeling of them.

Looking out of the cab's window, I tried to take everything in. I'm not sure what captivated me more, the cobblestone pavements, or the fact there was no one - people nor animals, not even a pigeon - on the streets. I had come from Mumbai, a city that never sleeps, where even at 2 am there is activity on every street corner in the city.

"Susuma, where is everyone?" I asked.

"What do you mean?" he said pointing out of the window, the old-looking streetlights illuminating the snow as it fell on London's famous landmarks.

"Where's the Queen and the people marching down the streets with the fuzzy hats?" I asked. Susuma laughed at me, but I was dead serious. He stopped chuckling when he saw my face. "Oh, ahh... she's probably sound asleep," he said, nodding solemnly.

It's funny how warped our perception of certain places and things can be. Over the years it seemed I'd eaten far too many British biscuits, wrapped in red and blue with pictures of Buckingham Palace's guards.

My freezing cold feet made it near impossible for me to fall asleep that first night at the YMCA hostel. I tried layering the socks I had packed from Mumbai, but they were thin, cotton ones and didn't help much. It seemed most of the clothes I had packed were inadequate. I had packed about 70 kilograms worth of luggage, which now seemed excessive, maybe even pointless, as I had not thought to research what clothes I would need, as I was arriving in winter.

Regardless, when I woke up the next morning, I felt a growing sensation of excitement. I was in London! While it was still not entirely light outside, I jumped into the shower, cherishing the tingling sensation of my toes warming up in the warm water.

Wearing five pairs of socks, I crammed my feet into the biggest (well, only) boots I had brought with me and set out on my first adventure abroad; it was time to find a way to call home and let them know I had arrived safely.

I had been told to get a 'Lebara' international calling card. I stepped outside to embark on a hunt for one of those, and very quickly decided I would need thicker and warmer socks. I visited a few stores, but I felt awkward and uneasy. Even though I could see many people from different cultural backgrounds, I still felt like a fish out of water. I thought I could feel everyone's eyes on me, but I later learnt it takes a lot more to get noticed in London.

It was incredible - the people, the streets, the blend of historic and modern architecture and two-storey houses, the accents, the multiple languages, the maps, even the traffic - so polite and orderly with just a light touch of a horn. I quickly learned that you could only cross the street at pedestrian crossings and that a red light really meant a red light.

I had explored different parts of India by myself many times but exploring London on that first day made me feel as if I'd just arrived on Mars. I could not relate to anything that I saw, felt or smelled.

Searching for something familiar, I stumbled upon a tiny corner shop run by an Indian, 'one of my own.' I scanned the shelves, taking in the colourful candy wrappers and magazines. I read the newspaper headlines; "Blair warns of 'serious trouble' on gas emissions." "Roof collapses on German supermarket" and "Student paper pulped over Mohammed cartoon."

I bought one of the 5 pound Lebara calling cards that give you 300 minutes - this was the mid-2000s, when mobile phones and mobile roaming were still very much reserved for the rich, and there were pay phones on every corner for the public to use.

I excitedly rushed into one of the renowned red telephone booths, marvelling at another movie moment. I followed the instructions on the calling card and punched the landline number, then the card PIN number. I was told the balance, and then I punched Father's number.

That excitement was short-lived however, as my call cut out within five minutes. It could have been frustration from jetlag or being cheated by a man from India, but I was enraged – and I went back to the store.

"You cheated me, my first day in London and you cheated me!" my voice cut through the shop's hustle and bustle instantly.

"Young man, please calm down," he said, raising his hands to try and calm me. But I'd already caused a scene.

"You told me 300 minutes! I used the telephone booth and I only got five minutes. My first day in London and I had to call my family, and this is what happens!"

My shouting was verging on hysteria, and I tried my best to fight back tears. People shook their heads and gave him disapproving looks as they left the store empty handed to avoid the drama.

"Okay okay, young man, you can use my landline, okay? You can't use this card on a pay phone, only on a landline," he said, ushering me into the back of the store.

His name was Sanjay bhai - bhai means brother in Hindi - and he was the first BBCD I met. A BBCD stands for British Born Confused Desi, a term coined by the Indian community in Britain to describe the second generation of Indians there. That fight actually laid the foundation for our long-standing friendship and his corner shop became somewhat of an anchor for me during my first weeks in London. He not only let me use his phone every week, free of charge, but I also made a habit of hanging around for a bit to chat, as he kept tending to his customers behind the till. I would often stand there helping him out, just wanting company, looking for a friend.

And I really needed a friend. Alone in a new country, away from everything you've ever known, for the first time in your life, can be incredibly scary - no matter how tough you are.

No amount of fisticuffs in the streets of Rajkot could prepare me for the battle with loneliness in London. I was optimistic at first - Father had so many friends in London, I had seen that for myself, enjoying their gifts of English biscuits and Bounty chocolates as I showed them around Mumbai in my little Fiat car. But I very quickly realised there are really two kinds of people in this world - givers and takers. "We're busy this week," most people said.

There was one family in particular that Father had encouraged me to seek out. They had come to see us in Mumbai many times before, and I always made it a point to give them the best experience possible when they visited. Soon after finding my feet in London, I reached out to them, proudly announcing my arrival. These were the same people for whom my father and I had dropped everything when they visited Mumbai, whom we picked up and dropped off at the airport after spending days looking after them. Naturally, I was looking forward to seeing them on 'their turf' and having them show me the city, spending time in their home and hopefully, enjoying a home-cooked Indian meal.

That expectation soon faded; every time they cancelled or put off the visit to another date in the future, saying, "next weekend would be better."

I now know that it is preferable to use public transport instead of taking cars due to expensive road tolls and heavy traffic, but when we finally found a Saturday that suited everyone, I felt somewhat offended when they told me to take a bus to reach their house, especially given how well we treated them when they visited Mumbai.

Cultural differences aside, this experience made me feel really alone. Looking back on it today it was another lesson learnt; never expect the same treatment you have given others. And, sometimes, your own people can be the first to let you down.

The President of the Indian Community Association did however stand by me, and I was lucky to have found him. He lent me a warm black winter coat - the perfect shield for London's icy gusts of wind – and he helped me find somewhere more permanent than the YMCA to live. He found me a room; a single bed in the loft in the roof of a house, also home to almost 15 people. There was one tiny bathroom for everyone to share. I had come from a country packed full of people, but even this was too much! I could kiss my cherished long bathroom visits goodbye. I stayed there for one night, and even that was one night too many.

The next day I called the president and after inquiring with about 20 different advertisements, we found another place to stay. It was slightly more expensive but peaceful and homely. I would have enough space and a flatmate; a quiet, young man from Sri Lanka. The location of the apartment was perfect. It was on the corner of Hounslow East train station, close to both the airport and my university. As I was going to study airline and airport management, I thought this would be a good thing.

I was slowly making my way through my arrival checklist (visiting family friends was one item I had scratched off long ago in annoyance) and now that accommodation was sorted, it was time to focus on my university studies.

Arriving at the university on my first day, I was struck by the sheer size of the campus. It consisted of several buildings that were wide and not tall like the schools I had attended in India. It had a grand reception area just like you see in the movies and the class rooms themselves looked like theatres!

It's funny how you can be speaking the same language, but an accent makes all the difference. I soon found that I struggled to understand what most people were saying to me. English still being quite new to me (especially one without a heavy Indian accent), I started to sit in the front row so I could read the lips of my British lecturers. I was trying very hard to make sense out of their thick accents (without much gesticulation or head-bobbing to guide me along, and no subtitles either). Not only that, but there were English accents from all over the world; the Chinese English accent, the South African English accent, the Spanish English accent, and Polish English accent... it was very hard to keep up!

Soon I wanted to go home, but in the back of my mind I was reminded of all the sacrifices my family had made for me to complete my studies in London. I was beginning to worry that I would fail my studies.

I was not as savvy in the English language as I thought I was, and so my first challenge was to actually understand what on earth everyone was talking about. Not only that, but all the references were grounded in local contexts too.

"So, let's say, class, Richard Branson walks into a Tesco and approaches the customer service desk..."

Who? My first thought was this Richard guy was maybe Britain's equivalent of that Bollywood star I'd used as a pin up boy during my RIMS campaign. And Tesco? It sounded expensive, like a fancy restaurant. I imagined lines of candlelit tables laid with crisp white cloths, and waiters dressed in penguin suits serving the finest foods on silver platters.

Those first few weeks of lectures went over my head. That familiar overwhelming feeling washed over me again. I felt out of my depth, just like I did at RIMS, but this time I was drowning, and it felt like I was millions of kilometres away from any support.

I was, however, in the same boat as many others. Thames Valley University was a melting pot of cultures and ideas from all corners of the world. And I was no longer the oldest in the class. I was surrounded by so many mature students in their 40s and 60s.

It was nice to have a 'community' with which to do things. The international students' hub arranged a tour for all of us 'freshers' and soon enough we'd visited all the sights. We saw the London Eye, Buckingham Palace and many other landmarks while zipping around in London's signature red double decker buses.

But once the initial excitement wore off, a sensation of loneliness started to set in. I was a long way from home, and it was hard to schedule a good time to call my family.

It became harder to ignore those long stretches of deafening silence, which were as commanding as the constant chimes of Big Ben.

After a while, I began to make friends with other international students, and the university staff too. I slowly created my own London family and started a network independent of my father's friends. I was building connections with people in the same boat as I was, and these good friends helped me when I was missing my family back in India.

One of my group assignments summed up this new feeling perfectly. After a suggestion from one of my classmates, we called our presentation "Insaniyat" meaning humanity in both Turkish and Hindi. I can't remember the point of the assignment or what the lecturer expected from us, but I know we wore our 'traditional' attire - an array of colours and patterns from India, Mauritius, the Philippines and more.

And perhaps this was the best part about Insaniyat - we were all so different, but we were all human. Underneath it all, we were all the same, dealing with similar feelings of missing home and wanting to impress our families who had given up so much for us to be there.

I would still visit Sanjay bhai in his shop on most days, but it wasn't enough to satisfy that longing for home. The worst part was that I couldn't even comfort myself with food! The university's offerings of lukewarm potato chips and mushy baby carrots were no match for the explosive flavours and satisfying variety of Indian cooking.

In London, a packet of tomato sauce was your best weapon against blandness, and everything was so expensive. Back home, 85 rupees - the equivalent of 1 pound or 2 Australian dollars - could get you a meal fit for a king. In London, that wouldn't even pay for a chocolate chip cookie from Tesco. By the way, I had finally learned what Tesco was - to think I believed it was a fine dining restaurant!

At one point I thought, maybe this really is my karma at work, a reprisal for giving everyone so much trouble back home. In India it is common to have domestic help regardless of wealth or social status. Families have people to help with cooking, sweeping and laundry. I thought back to how I would trouble the cook we had at home and demand roti straight from the tawa - the Indian equivalent of a flat frying pan or skillet - to my plate at dinner time. Or how I would complain if the curry had too much salt or not enough salt, was too bland or too spicy. Little did I know then how good my life had been.

It was hard not to think that every day was worse than the one before. I had made some new friends, but I still missed home. The real low point was my 25th birthday, one month after I had arrived. In India, a birthday is a huge celebration, a day of relatives and friends fussing over you and spoiling you with presents and food, often cutting a cake at midnight. But most importantly, you are surrounded by loved ones. But here I was, battling with a frozen pizza, that ended up burnt because I didn't know how to use the oven. The crust was charcoal, the middle was cold and with wind and rain pelting down my window, I felt miserable – I threw the pizza away and with a sigh, went to bed early.

Maybe London wasn't for me.

My Key Takeaways

- Only pack essentials and precious mementos: you can buy a lot of day-to-day items wherever you are heading and often more suited to your destination's lifestyle and climate. Don't make the same mistake as I did with socks! Research the climate of the place you are moving to.
- Don't rely on friends who have visited you in your own country. It is likely you will be disappointed.
- Build a second family: surround yourself with likeminded people, whether it be fellow international students or people you meet through special interest groups, or work. This creates a network of support in your new town and will help to lessen the feelings of homesickness and loneliness.
- Go on tours and participate in the social events organised by the university. These help you make friends as soon as possible.

Chapter 5

Cultural Shocks And Bob Marley

"Our cultural strength has always been derived from our diversity of understanding and experience."
– Yo-Yo Ma

Food is one of the greatest comforts in the world and one of the easiest ways to transport you to another place - even when you are miles away from home. Maybe that's due to its ability to activate all the senses. Or simply because, all biases aside, Indian food is the most delicious in the world!

Perhaps one of the biggest elements of any culture is food. When you have spent your whole life in one country and move to another, it can be one of the biggest culture shocks. My nickname 'Fook Fook' and introduction to other slang words was only just the beginning of learning about culture. I was still fairly sheltered back then - even with the world at my fingertips, those cyber chats had only been windows into western society and could not prepare me for the massive cultural differences around every corner. Some were shocking, others surprising, and most, like discovering Bob Marley, so very rewarding. But more about him later. First, I needed to satisfy my hunger with a slice of home. I craved naan and rotis and hearty curries... not these cheese and tomato sandwiches that seemed to be a staple at every corner shop.

As a traveller I wanted to try new things. I tried my best to strike a balance between the new and classic Indian comforts, which was made even harder by the fact that I was a vegetarian. I had not thought food would be a problem and the lack of Indian cuisine would cause me so much grief. I had clearly taken India's smorgasbord of flavours for granted and being vegetarian, my options in the UK were limited.

The university had a cafeteria and coffee shops were never more than a block away, but they didn't tickle my fancy at all. The food was quite the opposite to Indian cuisine; simple, bland and sometimes downright soggy.

I had sampled several types of canned foods and other ready-made items, but was scared off once and for all when my roommate told me that the packet of pasta sauce I was about to pour over my spaghetti contained animal products!

In India, there's a small symbol that indicates if an item is completely vegetarian or not: a green square with a circle in it if it is vegetarian, and a red square with a circle in it if it isn't. Without these symbols to guide me, I had to read every single label while doing my shopping to make sure it didn't contain eggs, fish, animal colouring agents or anything else that I was not supposed to eat.

Once or twice, I bought items that you would think would surely not contain any animal products, only to discover they in fact did.

Did you know pepper sauce can contain animal products? Neither did I.

I was tired of this, which motivated me to find a sustainable and appetising place to get food. At first, I would visit the nearest

Sikh temple and eat at least one wholesome meal every day. Sikh temples, or Gurudvaras, are located across the globe, and all of them have a community kitchen, where dinner is served every day. Their faith tells them that no one should go hungry while there are Sikhs around, and all who want to can come to the temples, regardless of religion, social status, age or gender. If you're living abroad and want to try something different, attend the prayers. Make sure to adhere to the rules such as covering your head and try and keep your mind open. Besides the free food, you might gain a valuable life lesson on other cultures.

I would donate a pound or two and pray for a job so I could give 5 next time. While the temple was great, I was hoping to find a place closer to home. Soon I found one, a restaurant run by a Punjabi family, called Galaxy Cuisine. It was located just around the corner from the train station, and I had walked past it a few times on my way to and from the university.

It wasn't a fancy place, but it had ample seating and a big counter filled with rotis, naan breads, curries, rice and sweets. This was heaven, I thought. But there was a catch - it was quite expensive, and I was yet to secure a part-time job. I was still converting pounds into rupees for every little thing I saw, denying myself most things as I could not believe the low value for money. So as Indians and especially Gujaratis do, I tried to barter with them.

The bell over the door chimed as I walked in. I saw an old man, sporting a blue turban and glasses, behind the counter, sitting on a stool with a newspaper folded in his lap. He looked up when I walked in and greeted me with a 'namaste' and a friendly smile.

"Sat Sri Akaal, uncle ji," I replied, returning his namaste in the customary way Sikhs greet each other

"How can I help you?" he asked, getting up from his stool, laying his hands on top of the glass counter.

I told him that I'd come from Mumbai to study and that I was finding it difficult to satisfy my cravings for good food.

"I promise to come here every day for my main meal, if you give me a good price," I stated. "Ahh, young man, we don't do that sort of thing here in London, this is the price," he said eyebrows raised, pointing to the board behind him.

"But I will be a repeat customer, guaranteeing you an income every day," I tried again.

"The price is the price," he retorted, standing firm while looking me in the eye. He must have been a BBCD, I thought, never having experienced the barter culture from our homeland.

"But I don't even need the standard serving, you can give me a smaller portion!" I suggested. He touched his turban, pressing his temple as if asking for strength, stroked his beard and looked me up and down before meeting my eye.

"I admire your persistence, young man," he said.

"Okay, come tomorrow, I will give you two big rotis and a curry for 5 pounds."

Either he admired my persistence, or just wanted to get rid of me. Nevertheless, as promised, the very next day I returned and was greeted by a different man in his place behind the counter, the restaurant owner's son.

I said I had spoken with his father the previous day, but he wouldn't give me the deal. I left the shop, head hung low, stomach rumbling and returned to the can of baked beans in my pantry.

I decided to try one more time and returned the next day. But it was the son again. I turned to leave but the father called out just as

I was about to open the door. "Give him the food, we have made a deal, he will now come every day," he said.

The son did not want to agree, and eyeing me, said, "This is not how to run a business, Papa!"

But his father was firm and would not budge, and soon the son begrudgingly put down a plate full of steaming hot curry, two freshly made rotis glistening with ghee (clarified butter) and a small bowl of fluffy rice in front of me. I leaned over the hot food and let the steam and the spices tickle my nose as I took a deep breath.

Finally, food was sorted!

With a full belly for the first time in what felt like years and with the prospect of enjoyable and filling daily meals, the next pressing challenge was landing a job.

Like most international students starting out, Father had given me money for daily expenses but that was capped at six months - from then on, I would have to pay my own way and my money was starting to run out.

Hanging around at the international student office, it wasn't long before I got my first job. Unlike in India where I pretty much would offer my services and start the next day, I had to be patient and wait until an opportunity opened. It didn't pay much, but it was a lot of fun - greeting international students at the airport.

I did what Susuma had done for me, introducing new arrivals to London and sharing my tips and tricks; "The first thing you need guys, is a selection of warm wool socks! Primark usually have good 'twofer' deals," I told them knowingly.

London was expensive and I soon realised I needed another source of income to live comfortably. I chased a few other customer service jobs and called in favours from some university friends, but being a vegetarian, I didn't want to work at fast food restaurants. I had never even touched a piece of meat in my life, let alone eaten any, and I was not about to start now.

I also wanted to be somewhere, where I felt I was learning and building on my skills, adding on to what they taught me at the university.

I picked up WebT@ntra again and got some website design projects on the side, but the pay wasn't enough to justify the valuable time it took away from my studies.

Summer break was coming up, which meant I was able to work unlimited hours under the student visa restrictions, so I needed something fast. But rejection was rife. I was getting nowhere.

I had previously been warned about the traditional tikka I put on my forehead every day. In Hinduism, the red dot of vermilion paste applied between the eyebrows or in the middle of your forehead signifies the centre of wisdom and concentration, home to the third eye and it was something I had done my entire life as part of my morning ritual.

It was also something I was adamant on keeping, regardless of anyone's advice to not make myself look different. I had heard many stories about young men and women moving abroad, who had thrown away all their values the first second they got a chance to. Before leaving Mumbai, my father asked me to stay true to my upbringing, to stay away from alcohol and cigarettes, to keep to a vegetarian diet and to be respectful to women. So for my tikka I settled for a compromise; instead of a big dot I started creating a thin, faded line.

I also started introducing myself as Neal instead of Nilesh. I mainly did this because it was easier for people to say than my name, but I guess it was also a way of making myself sound more familiar and British to potential employers. First name Neal, last name Mack.

Initially, I had my sights set on finding a job (any job) at the airport, where I could at least try to mingle with the staff and build some connections that might be useful in obtaining my degree, especially considering the compulsory practical experience required for my second year of studies. My course coordinator told me no international student would find work with an airline, due to security reasons, but I was determined to find something (anything)!

I printed hundreds of copies of my resume and took my friend from university and fellow Insaniyat member, Tugba along with me as she was also looking for a job. We teamed up and slipped our resumes under office doors at the airport in the hope that someone would notice us.

Eventually, a cafe owner noticed my resume, and offered me a one-week trial starting the very next day. They gave me a shirt with 'Neal' on a plastic badge, printed in front of me using their Dymo Label Maker. It wasn't what I'd been hoping for, but I thought that by being at the cafe I would meet people with airline jobs and eventually connect with my future employer.

But I never showed up.

The next morning, I got up at 5 am to get ready for the 6 am morning shift. I pulled the T-shirt over my head, straightened my name badge and walked to the door. I looked at the door. I opened the door. But I was not able to get out of the door... Something was holding me back. I might have needed a job – I was desperate for one. But this wasn't where I wanted to start. I realised if I went to work at the cafe that morning, I would risk becoming stuck there.

In a split second I decided I would make another attempt at getting a slightly better job. I was naive in thinking too much of the bigger picture, without realising that sometimes it's the little steps along the way that can help you get there. Even jobs that we think we may be overqualified for.

I resolutely kicked off my shoes, locked the door and tossed the T-shirt in the trash on my way back to bed thinking I'd get a better airport job soon enough. I realise now that you should never turn your nose up at something you may consider 'beneath you' because of your experience in your home country - everything can provide a chance for learning if you let it. The trick is to work it to your benefit, and to move on at the right time.

Summer break was coming up and the first batch of assignments had been handed in. I continued to look for a job so I could support myself when my allowance ran out. It was never an option for me to ask for more money, as I had clearly been told that after the first semester I would be on my own. I realised I needed to look outside the airport and shortly after sending out my resume and filling out applications left, right and centre an opportunity came up with the multinational brand Marks & Spencer, which I grabbed with both hands.

I passed the initial customer service screening test with the help of a friend, another international student who had landed a job at Marks & Spencer just months earlier. I was invited for a face-to-face interview with the company's Head of Human Resources for the next stage of the interview process.

The position was in Watford, a two-and-a-half-hour trip from London via two trains and a bus. Wanting to make a good impression and ensuring I arrived early I decided to book the direct bus from the airport that cost 20 pounds. But that was almost a week's worth of meals for me. I just couldn't afford it. And so, for the first time in my life I borrowed money from my roommate.

I had never borrowed any money before, and it wasn't something I'd ever seen my father do. I felt very uncomfortable taking the 50 pound note from him and I promised I'd pay him back as soon as I could.

I arrived at the mall significantly ahead of time, while it was still closed. The security guard pointed me to a coffee shop opposite the mall, suggesting I wait there. It was a small but cosy coffee shop, with tiny tables dressed in red checked tablecloths and wooden chairs neatly arranged around them, and most importantly - it was a warm place to wait.

The HR manager was to come there to pick me up, and take me to the formal interview in the mall's offices. An hour later I noticed her crossing the street, leaning forward a little to brace herself against the cold. She was wearing a heavy coat and the bell over the door tinkled as she entered the coffee shop. I stood up and greeted her and asked if she'd like a coffee first. She happily accepted my offer and I showed her to my table by the window where she freed herself from her coat and hung it over the back of her chair.

I didn't have much money of my own, but here I was buying her a coffee. I carefully arranged the coffee, milk, two types of sugar and a couple of small biscuits on a tray with some napkins and a glass of water and placed it in front of her. We sat for about half an hour and chatted about everyday things while she finished her coffee, holding it with both hands to warm up her cold fingers.

The biscuits seemed to go down well too, and she asked me if I had settled down well in London, how student life was treating me, why I had chosen aviation and what I had been doing before I decided to move all the way from India to the UK.

She told me her daughter was studying web design and I ended up sharing some of my experiences from my days as a web designer in Mumbai. After a very pleasant and relaxed conversation we made our way up to the office, and she asked me to sit down and wait.

Twenty minutes later she emerged, heels click-clacking towards me with every step (another cultural difference I was yet to understand - women in India had it far easier in flats!) She was holding a clipboard, eyes scanning the pages. She turned the clipboard towards me with a pen attached.

"Congrats, you've got the job, Neal!" she said.

On the clipboard was my contract of employment, ready to sign.

"But what about the interview?" I thought aloud. "You already passed the test," she said.

"I don't understand..." I questioned, puzzled.

"Well, this is a customer service job and you've already proven how capable you are of delivering good service. The way you presented the coffee on the tray, you didn't assume I'd take white or brown sugar with my coffee, and you also served it with a glass of water and something to eat. That was a very nice touch, and it all came naturally to you. You also held a conversation with ease, which is an important trait to have as a customer service agent, so you have already shown your worth. No need for further questioning!"

The experience made me realise that a good first impression can transcend cultural differences - at the heart of every good impression is presentation, whether it is wearing a suit, which helped get me the job with Cipla or simply serving coffee to the HR manager.

Training started the very next week. We learnt about the different customer service methods. Marks & Spencer's service style focused on empathy. It flipped some of my own ingrained sales ideologies on their head.

I sat in the training course, contemplating some of these tactics, thinking of all the times I'd said, 'sorry to keep you waiting' in various other jobs. If only I'd said, 'thank you for waiting,' maybe I would have received more business.

Besides language and food, music can vary greatly from country to country.

Soon after starting my job at Marks & Spencer, or 'M&S,' I encountered the music of the legendary Bob Marley for the first time.

I was stationed in the homewares department and a customer approached the desk to enquire about a specific clock.

"I want the Bob Marley clock," he said, matter-of-factly, pulling two twenty-pound notes out of his wallet.

"Sorry, sir?" I asked, racking my brain.

Was Bob Marley a specific brand? Maybe it was a style or colour? How did I not know this? I had felt so comfortable just twenty minutes earlier educating a couple about our range of kettles. I tried to remember my training and followed the man's gaze, realising he was referring to the clocks on the wall behind me. There was Princess Diana's smiling face, Donald Duck and a few other cartoon characters. We did have one previously of a man with dreadlocks, it had sold out a few days earlier, which I never did quite understand, because I had no idea who he was.

"The brightly coloured one with the dark man with long hair?" I asked.

"Yes, that's the one," he replied curtly.

He was getting very restless and seemed annoyed, which threw me off a little. Did he have somewhere to be right now or a bus to catch? Trying to provide good service, I handed him a pen and paper and asked him to write down the name, so I could look it up in our system.

His cheeks flushed and he let out a flabbergasted breath as he took the pen and slammed it down on the desk.

At the time I couldn't understand why this man was so upset about a specific clock with the face of a long-haired man, I could only assume that most other people hadn't heard of him either, given that I hadn't.

"Thank you. I can see here sir that we are sold out, I can order it in for you and put it aside for pick up..." I trailed off realising the man had stalked off in a huff.

What a funny man, why was he so upset? I found my floor manager and told her the story of this strange customer interaction.

"You don't know Bob Marley?" she squealed.

"... Should I?" I shrugged.

She shook her head, "Let's talk later but next time just nod your head and smile, okay?" I went home and told my housemate Raj. His reaction was the same.

"You don't know Bob Marley!" he said in shock.

"How is it that everyone knows this Bob guy with messy long hair? Why is he so important?" I said, exasperated. I didn't like not knowing things. I'd been made fun of my whole life for 'not knowing.' Now it seemed the teasing had followed me to London, and I didn't appreciate it one bit.

Raj returned moments later with a CD.

"This, this is Bob Marley," he said, handing it to me.

The melody was very different to anything I had heard before, so different to the static-like beats of India, notes so smooth and long. I listened to Buffalo Soldier on repeat in my room for two weeks, letting the groovy rhythm take over my body. I was dancing like a monkey in my small room. More than once, I bumped my knee on my bed or knocked my elbows on the walls, but it was worth it. Where had Bob Marley been all my life?

It was enough to drive Raj mad and one day he stormed into my room and snatched his CD back. But luckily for me YouTube had even more Bob Marley songs than were on the CD. So unfortunately for Raj, the Bob Marley dance sessions continued for the rest of my tenancy. And I have been hooked ever since.

That first encounter with Bob Marley in the homewares department at Marks & Spencer was a real eye opener to cultural differences. The 'unknown' can lay the perfect foundations for misunderstanding. Something significant in our own cultures may not be appreciated in another's, simply because of a lack of understanding, or in my case, a lack of knowledge.

The realisation hit me a few weeks later, when our shipment of additional Bob Marley clocks finally arrived. For this man, my not knowing of Bob Marley was the equivalent of him not knowing about Hanuman. I had deeply offended him without even intending to.

But needless to say, I got a Bob Marley clock, too.

I made a conscious effort after this to attend more international student events, so I could learn even more about people's cultures, interests and traditions. It wasn't long before I realised I had some prejudices.

The only place I'd encountered dark skinned people before coming to London was in the multiplex at Juhu. Bollywood movies would cast dark skinned people as gangsters and drug addicts and perpetuate stereotypes about other races. I learned so much about how friendly, interesting, and unique people from different countries can be.

My view on people with disabilities changed completely after I arrived in London, too. It started with crosswalks for visually impaired pedestrians. I noticed the tactile paving, that is the dots on the sidewalks, at the traffic light intersections and pedestrian crossings. Being in a country where snow and sleet would make the ground slippery in winter, I assumed they were there to stop people from slipping into the road and being run over. I was walking back to the university one rainy day after grabbing a coffee with Tugba in between lectures. I was wearing sneakers and I nearly slipped.

"Good thing these dots are on the ground," I said, chuckling. "That could've been a nasty fall."

"You know they're a hazard warning for people that can't see well, right?" Tugba asked.

I was blown away at the efforts made to include everyone in society. In India, when I was growing up, people with disabilities were treated quite badly. Everyone believed they had done something wrong or bad in a previous life and were being punished for it. Many were on the streets, living their lives as beggars, but there is more awareness now, although there is definitely a long way to go.

I started to pay more attention to people around me and understand the principles of multiculturalism and inclusivity. I noticed the special arrangements for people with disabilities; the small elevators next to staircases, the ramps, the push buttons next to doors and the sound the green man made at pedestrian crossings. No-one was really treated differently, and everyone was given support. I would not look at people with disabilities in the way I used to ever again.

Soon after, I stumbled on the opportunity to help raise funds for the National Autistic Society and I eagerly volunteered. I proudly put on the 'Action for Autism' T-shirt they gave me and collected more money than any other student. I stood on the same corner for two days holding out my charity collection tin and handing out brochures with information about autism.

I also noticed how many international students often stuck to their own kind. While I too found comfort in speaking Hindi and eating Indian food, I also saw the value and importance of branching out. I didn't want to only socialise within my own cultural circle and form a 'little India' in another place. I still can't help but wonder, if this was how the 'real world' operated and feel that if we spent more time with people we don't understand, maybe we would experience less hate and conflict.

I soon found my stride in my new job at M&S. It was hard being on my feet all day and even though I spent five hours commuting, I really enjoyed serving customers and learning about different appliances in the homewares department.

But no matter how busy I was, I still often thought about family. The smallest things, like a smell, an image or a sound can remind you of someone or invoke a memory of something from back home.

One day, as I was folding bras I thought, imagine if Maneck Aunty could see me now! Here I was, an Indian boy packing away women's undergarments and swimwear daily. She'd be shocked!

You see, the homewares department bordered the lingerie department and I'd never seen so much lace in my life! Not even back in that computer lab in Mumbai where I'd discovered more than western swear words. I am chatty by nature and soon the lingerie customers, mostly older women, started coming to my desk to be served. It was nice to have so many people to chat to about all sorts of things, and it gave me an opportunity to improve my English.

It wasn't long before I was reassigned to work in the lingerie department.

One day an elderly customer told me I'd been folding the bras all wrong, placing both cups over one another to form a ball.

"No, no, no! darling, you must be new to this, you're doing it all wrong," she wagged her finger at me and reached over the counter, taking the bra-ball out of my hands.

"See, just like this," she folded one cup inside the other.

"These aren't to carry a ball - women don't have balls, we have breasts!" she exclaimed, finger pointed knowingly, chest puffed out, with her voice cutting through the chatter in the store.

The words lingered awkwardly above the silence before a few giggles erupted nearby.

Then both of us started laughing, the kind of laughter that comes from a pure place, and I felt grateful for this woman who had taught me something without being condescending or making me feel small.

Aside from my friendly conversations with customers, I was becoming very good at selling the M&S More credit card. The card was considered the hardest product in the history of the company to push, and each department was set a Key Performance Indicator, or KPI, to sign up at least five new members each week.

That KPI target was never met - until I came along.

It was my chatting with the older ladies that did it.

My success made me feel I was back in Rajkot. I was finally completely at ease, as if I was riding my bike and selling my sandwich makers.

But the three-month summer vacation was coming to an end.

I loved Marks & Spencer (and the pay!) but I just didn't know how I was going to sustain a full university workload with a job and long commute. I knew I needed to leave and find something more convenient, so when the university reopened, I asked my teachers to put in a good word for me with the administration. I was soon offered a job on campus as a technician in the IT department, my experience with computer hardware in India paid off and I left M&S (and retail for that matter) for good.

My Key Takeaways

- It would be a good idea to learn some basic cooking before you leave: making dishes from your country can help ease some of the feelings of missing home.
- Be easy on yourself when learning new things and adjusting to cultural differences, it will take time.
- Whether you're a student or a migrant, whenever you arrive in a new country, check out the best budget stores - the first few years might be tight, so it's good to know where to get what! This goes for groceries, too.

- Always make sure that you pay attention to details and what other people may appreciate – it was the way I served coffee that got me the job at M&S.
- Always be open to suggestions and learn to laugh at yourself - many Indians find this difficult.

Chapter 6

Home Is Not A Place, It's A Feeling

"Giving up smoking is the easiest thing in the world. I know because I have done it thousands of times."

– Mark Twain

I was finding the coursework at university very challenging. Maneck Aunty tried to round up a few remote tutors to help me out, but it was difficult. That feeling of overwhelming anxiety was building up again. No matter how hard I tried, aviation theory just flew over my head.

I made some new friends, settled into university life, and had the extra comfort of eating regular, traditional Indian cuisine, but I still felt a longing for home.

One of my favourite Indian traditions and holidays is Diwali. You could even say I enjoy it more than my own birthday.

Diwali is an annual five-day festival of lights, which brings together millions of Hindus, Sikhs, and Jains. All over the world people celebrate new beginnings, a new year, and the victory of light over darkness. I tried calling Father's friends again thinking they might invite me to join their Diwali celebrations. But no one asked me to join them for a meal or even a cup of tea. Honestly, it was the most miserable Diwali I had experienced in my life.

That feeling was enough to trigger the all-consuming loneliness and homesickness all over again. I was tired from all the hard work I was doing; the studies were difficult, and the weather was cold and miserable.

It's not easy to stick things out alone. Sometimes, you need more than words down the end of a telephone line, or a video call on a screen to comfort you. So, when I flew back to Mumbai a few weeks later for my brother's wedding, I booked a one-way ticket.

After nine months, I was done with London. It was time to return home where I felt most comfortable, and which perhaps, I should never have left at all.

Landing on home turf, I instantly felt at ease, it was as if all my worries and concerns that I had in London disappeared as soon as the aeroplane's wheels hit the tarmac.

Seeing my family's smiling faces again after months (which felt like years), I cried with happiness and relief.

It was the longest I had ever been away, and I was so glad to be back.

Everyone was excited about my return and my brother's wedding. I revelled in celebration after celebration (a traditional Indian wedding can last a good seven days), enjoying great company and finally, a real hearty home cooked meal.

I began to wonder why I had ever wanted to leave Mumbai in the first place. Everything here was familiar, it was comfortable, it was safe. My money could stretch further in Mumbai than it ever could in London. And the best part? I would never have to eat lukewarm chips, burnt pizzas or soggy carrots again.

In Mumbai I had built a successful website business from the ground up and I still had those contacts. As I watched my family dance and laugh at one of my brother's many wedding functions, I felt that I could easily put my London life behind me and start afresh in Mumbai.

I confided in Maneck Aunty about my negative experiences. She had spent a year in France in her youth and was empathetic because she had been in similar situations herself. She would tell tales from her own travel days, sharing the same stories for the umpteenth time, but I never minded hearing them again (and still don't). My favourite story was from the seventies, when she and her friend hitchhiked to London from France, camping in a tent along the way. Imagine doing something like that today!

My brother lent me his ear as often as he could, too.

"We told you it was going to be hard, bhai," he said after I had complained extensively about the bland British food one evening during a meal at home.

"You'll be a football forever, bouncing from one thing to another, but that's okay, as long as you're happy."

I looked down at the ring on my finger that Phiroze Uncle had left me before he passed away, remembering how he spoke of 'football' as something positive.

I made my choice. I was coming home.

It took me a few days to muster the courage to tell Father, though.

I chose the night before the wedding, an evening dedicated to traditional dancing and games, where the mood was festive and cheerful. The perfect environment for my news to be received well.

Or so I thought.

"Father, I'm coming home," I said smiling.

"Yes? You are here already, beta, you are home," he said, laughing as if I had pointed out the obvious.

"What I mean is, I'm going to come home forever. I'm done with London, and I am ready to continue my life here," I said, thinking he would be delighted with the prospect of his son returning home for good.

I was very, very wrong.

"What? You are not wasting this opportunity!" he said angrily, arms flailing.

"We have supported you so much for your dream! It was you who convinced us it was the right thing for you, and we have provided so much money and help for you to live in London. You cannot give up now. I will not allow it, and that's final!"

"But Father, I am miserable in London, my studies are difficult, it rains all the time, people are hard to understand, no one visits me, or even allows me to visit them! I'm lonely and even the food is terrible!" I whimpered, close to tears.

When you're in a bad place, it's funny how your perspective can be hijacked by anything and everything that's wrong. I was blinded to the positives, like my university friends, my job or my apartment that I actually enjoyed very much. In India, it was never possible for me to get the sleep that I wanted, as you have to get up when everyone else gets up. But I was so homesick, I could only think of everything that made me miserable.

"These are all things you can change," he said, folding his arms.

"Most of all, I just miss everyone and everything about Mumbai, and India!" I said imploringly, scanning his face for any sign of understanding. "I don't want to have to leave again."

"Just because you miss something, Nilesh, doesn't mean that it's right for you," he said. I knew the discussion was over.

I felt slightly defeated as he wrapped his arms around me, my dream of a new Mumbai life squashed in his embrace.

Thanks to reassuring words from my brother and Maneck Aunty, I knew I would never really be alone. They all wanted me to succeed, and I could not abandon the journey I had set for myself.

I had to go back and finish what I had started. And I had to do it by myself.

In India - as in many places - life's progression is very much thought of as linear: go to school, go to high school, get a job/attend university, find a partner (by yourself or through your parents), get married, have children... and the circle of life starts again.

For centuries in India it has been a tradition for parents and the family to choose a partner for their children and while 'self-arranged' or 'love-arranged' marriages have become more popular over time, a significant number of marriages in India are still arranged by parents. My own family was worried about me being lonely in a new country and thought that having company would do me a world of good, so they tried to arrange a marriage for me.

I knew my family's actions were coming from a good place, but I had no intention of settling down at a time in my life when I felt the whole world was at my feet. I was just getting started, enjoying my independent student life and it was hard enough working on my own hopes and dreams, let alone considering someone else's. I wasn't ready.

Not wanting to disappoint Father, I still went along for a few meetings with the woman I might have married. But I knew before we met that it wasn't to be.

"Nilesh, how is it all going?" he asked one evening.

"Fine," I responded half-heartedly.

"I don't want to be responsible for someone's unhappiness, Nilesh, and I especially don't want to ruin two lives by taking her away from her family to a new country where she will know no one and worse, have a husband who doesn't love her," he said.

Father understood that you can help to guide someone in a direction, but then the magic is up to them. The match was cancelled, and I would return to London by myself.

There's a reason people say 'get out of your comfort zone.' It's the experiences that challenge us the most that truly put us to the test.

"That's fine little brother, just quit," my brother said to me when he got wind of my conversation with Father.

"It's the easy option to quit, you know, why take the harder path? Who cares about all the time and effort that's already been invested into London, right?"

The reverse psychology worked wonders on me. My family knew what made me tick: proving people wrong.

After the wedding, I packed my suitcase (I travelled much lighter this time!) arrived at Mumbai Airport, passed through the boarding gates, and waved goodbye to my family once more.

I tried my best to take off the rose-tinted glasses I'd put on when I landed in Mumbai, and instead focus on the task at hand: excelling in my studies and making London a great experience. Because I'm no quitter.

Sitting in the aeroplane on the way back to London, I started making a new list in my head, a plan of attack. With roughly ten hours of travel time to kill, I could take my time.

I needed a new job, which was a big one to check off, and it would ideally have to be something close to my apartment. The challenge of food was only partly solved, the small portions at the Punjabi restaurant in Hounslow just weren't quite hitting the spot. But until I figured something out, I decided not to worry about it. I would eat the food I could get my hands on and be content for the time being. It was just sustenance, after all.

Making my list was momentarily interrupted when a crew member handed me the inflight meal. And that's when it hit me - not just the waft of curry escaping from beneath the lid of the takeaway container, but the idea to create an Indian lunch box service!

Surely, I was not the only Indian missing my home cuisine in London. I could kill two birds with one stone – working and eating all the delicious food I could stomach.

In Mumbai they have tiffin services, or lunch box deliveries, where homemade meals are delivered to businesses for a small price. This was 2006 and although takeaway existed it wasn't exactly UberEATS-standard yet.

Within a few days of landing in London, I booked and launched the domain IndianTiffinServices.com and made a list of every Indian restaurant within a 20-mile radius of my apartment in Hounslow.

Then I did what I have always done best – sell.

Walking into the first restaurant on my list, I confidently asked to speak with the manager and pitched my idea with gusto.

"This could bring you more than 40 regular orders every day," I rattled off the start of my pitch to the prospective client.

"You already have the kitchen and the menu, you already have the staff, and you have your own delivery model, all you're missing is the online platform to connect you with more customers than ever before. I'll add your set menu to the website and people can call and order the packed meals 7 days in advance, buying for one week at the time."

"What's the catch?" the restaurateur enquired. "How much are you charging to list on this website and what about commission?"

"No fee, no commission," I said. "Just give me food in-kind for my services." That Indian tiffin service sustained me for a good four years. I maintained the website and paid the annual domain fee. It was very easy work. The menu rotated every 21 days, which meant I got a lot of variety.

I also gave meals to my room-mate Raj, and in return, he offered to pay for household essentials like dishwashing liquid, laundry detergent and toilet paper. So not only was I eating like a king, but thanks to the free meals and household products, I was watching my savings grow and grow. I was free to focus on university, work and my social life.

When university restarted, I managed to land a job at the ICT helpdesk in the university library and I also made an effort to become closer to my international friends, many of whom were exceptional at English and only too happy to help me out with mine. They taught me how to party, which soon became a Friday and Saturday night ritual. We would meet up in Trafalgar Square and decide where to go on a whim.

The bouncers and club owners came to know me very quickly as the crazy Indian who didn't drink but was always hitting the dance floor with a glass of, what I liked to call, 'H2O on the rocks.'

I stayed true to my values and did not touch alcohol, but it was better not to draw too much attention to myself by not having a drink in my hand. I added some ice cubes and a slice of lemon, and it looked just like any other drink. And my crazy monkey dancing was appreciated by other people on the dance floor, too.

"Oy, mate, you're wasted!" they would yell.

Little did they know. I never was.

Apparently, there is something attractive about someone dancing like an idiot because I soon understood what the western term 'chick magnet' was all about. Women would dance with me and we would have a great time, but after two or three dances they would want to get a drink. That's when I introduced them to my alcohol-drinking friends. It was a win-win for everybody.

Wheeling and dealing as always, I quickly came to an arrangement with the bouncers and club owners: if I brought a group of people with me, I wouldn't have to pay an entry fee.

That arrangement and enjoying water, meant a night out with friends would usually only cost me the bus or tube fare.

The clubs were great, but the casinos were the best - you didn't even have to pay an entry fee! Since I didn't drink or gamble (and still don't), I sat backed and watched while sipping my H2O on the rocks. Casinos are actually wonderful for many things, and I have used them as my office or study hall on more than one occasion. The temperature is just right, you get discounts at restaurants, and some even offer free coffee and sandwiches.

What I loved the most about partying in London was that even when it came to closing time in the clubs and pubs, celebrations continued in the streets. The city came alive with partygoers at 4 am, buskers beating drums, winding queues forming outside kebab shops and people continuing to dance and sing in the buses on the way home.

I got the feeling my life was changing, and that everything was settling into place - I wasn't worried about food, being alone on my birthday or missing India.

I started to move on and learn how to appreciate the good things about my new town, and the more opportunities it could bring.

About a year and a half into London, Father called me, and he wasn't happy that I no longer tried to connect with his friends in London, who had visited us so many times in Mumbai. I didn't have the heart to tell him about the cold shoulders, the voicemails, and the lack of interest. He started to worry about me and couldn't understand why I wasn't reaching out to our 'extended family'.

"Son, why are you not calling these people and going to their houses?" he pressed on.

I ignored the question and instead posed one of my own.

"Father, why don't you just come and visit me, see where I live and where I study for yourself?"

My father and sister eventually came round to the idea of coming to London. I was so excited to host them, but their visas were cancelled after an immigration agent in Mumbai completed the paperwork incorrectly.

I was so upset I let my anger get the better of me and threatened the agent on the phone. I wanted the agent to know how frustrated and terrible I felt that my family couldn't see me, but I remembered my time at RIMS. I remembered my decision to swap fists for brains. I hung up the phone. It was time to use my brains.

The next day I asked my course coordinator if he could write a letter addressed to my father, inviting him to visit the campus for an official tour. A few other university staff members agreed to write letters too. Getting travel visas in India can be hard work. Most people are blessed with passports that don't require tourist visas, or if they do, are easily granted upon application. In India, we will often have to show bank statements, tax returns, hotel bookings, return tickets, sometimes even letters from employers to show we have the means to sustain our adventures abroad. I booked a fancy hotel and first-class plane tickets for my family and sent these documents, and my bank account details to the immigration office. I had enough money to sponsor my family during their time here. The finishing touch? Reverse psychology, just like my brother had used on me.

I told Father exactly what to say at his immigration interview:

"Tell them you have no interest in visiting a horribly cold and grey country, but that your son won't stop pestering you to visit."

"As long as you don't kill us off again!" My sister said on the phone the night before the interview.

Post interview, Father was pleasantly surprised by my tactics.

"Sir, why do you want to come to London?" the officer had asked my father sternly.

"I don't want to visit London," Father told him.

"You don't?"

"That's right. London? It's not for me."

"So why are you here?"

"Look, I don't want to go to London, but my son studies and works there. It's his wish for me to come and see where he lives and see how he's doing. Every time we speak, he just won't let it rest. London, London, London."

"But what if he needs you? London is very far away! Sir, you must go, you must go and see your son."

And just like that, Father left the immigration office with a big stamp of approval for himself and for my sister.

Father's friends made contact when he arrived in London, but he soon faced the same behaviour as I had done. These people had busy lives, much too busy to carve out time to show him around the city.

He was a little saddened and realised I was right; people were not the same as they were in India.

At the time, I wasn't made of money - so I cancelled the hotel bookings and first-class tickets. But I still made sure my family had a good time. I gave them an official tour of the university campus and after that, I held a party at the student union hall and invited everybody I knew - we had a blast.

I had never felt so proud and accomplished since graduating from RIMS and I was so happy to share it with my father and sister.

I had one more surprise up my sleeve.

Two days before their flight back to Mumbai I told them to prepare for a day of adventure. I still had a tidy amount of savings and I wanted to do something extra special.

The limo arrived promptly at 9 am, taking us across London Bridge, past Big Ben, and the London Eye. I was buzzing from the high of seeing the smiles on their faces, which only grew wider when they discovered I had booked them a one-hour helicopter ride to see the River Thames, Buckingham Palace, Hyde Park, and the other sites of London from above.

I'll never forget the rush I got from seeing them light up, and I was proud I had made them happy. It was at that point I truly understood the expression, 'to feel at home'.

I discovered home was not just a physical place. It's a feeling. And while I couldn't resurrect my family home brick by brick, I could easily replicate the feelings of content you experience when you're home. I could now do this whether my family was in London with me or not.

Father stopped calling me after that trip. He had seen London first-hand, knew I was safe and that I was able to stand on my own two feet. He stopped asking me to visit his friends too.

But he didn't change the way he treated them or anyone else when they came to visit him in Mumbai. I didn't understand why until years later.

"I don't do tit-for-tat, beta," he told me.

"But why would you show such kindness and hospitality when they didn't do anything for me or for you?" I asked bluntly.

His reply was simple and true: "Because that's not how karma works."

And I could only hope I'd built up enough good karma, or at least, enough luck to help me tackle my next challenge: securing a job at Heathrow Airport.

My Key Takeaways

- Life is always going to throw challenges your way. Giving up may be easier and safer but persevering through the tough times is so much more rewarding. Set little goals for yourself, so the 'bigger picture' appears more achievable, and take little steps every day.

- Celebrate your wins: there's no point in being successful without sharing it and enjoying it. Just like the helicopter ride with Father and my sister, celebrating the wins can also be a way of showing gratitude to those who have helped you along the way.
- Socialise and make new friends. But don't forget who you are or deviate from your values. Peer pressure is not worth it.
- Be active in class. Participate and contribute, and never miss a lecture. The teacher, and your fellow students will remember you, and you will get more out of it.

Chapter 7

Terminal 4

"When things go wrong, don't go with them."
– Elvis Presley

Life can be very much like an airport departure lounge: you think you're ready to go to a gate and take off in one direction, but then at the last moment you may face changes or cancellations that force you to take another path.

I had many "flight cancellations" or "gate changes" in my pursuit to land an airline job. I applied for more than 350 jobs within a matter of weeks. Each time it felt as if my plane was being grounded or turned around, someone else's life flight taking precedence over mine. I began to second-guess myself; maybe my course coordinator had been right all along, that it would be impossible for me to find a job with an airline. Even before I had arrived in London, he and I had exchanged some terse emails.

As part of my course requirements, I had been told that I would need one year of practical experience, a so-called sandwich year in-between the second and fourth years of my honours degree.

That experience, he said, was near impossible to secure with any airline at Heathrow Airport as an international student. Let alone an international student in their first year of university. He concluded I would have to return to Mumbai for my practical component.

Why on earth would I travel halfway across the world and move my life to London, only to return to Mumbai for experience? I had an angry email typed, but I paused, took a deep breath, and reassessed.

He said it was near impossible, not entirely impossible.

I deleted the email, and I accepted the challenge.

With renewed gusto and determination, I continued pushing my CV under the doors of the offices of important airline personnel at Heathrow Airport. I had a little win, as I managed to land a casual job with Virgin Atlantic, helping people scan their tickets using newly introduced automated machines. While I had a great time working there, I continued to apply for other jobs. What I really hoped for was a part-time position with a larger, "high-flying" airline. I thought my chances were better than ever before as I already had "one foot in the door."

Over the next couple of months, I sat through 35 interviews, most consisting of an initial meet and greet and group exercises or exams. But I found it hard to connect one-on-one, as I was surrounded by people just as eager to please as I was.

When the 36th interview came along, I had no hope and went in with no expectations, but it turned out to be a lucky number for me.

The first stage involved a pre-interview examination of aviation terminology and calculations that would be conducted over a phone call. I have never been great with numbers.

This is useless, I thought.

Remember, that my brother had got married recently, well fortunately, my sister-in-law's brother, Nehit, lived in London, too, so I finally had some family around me. He was an accountant and he helped me out by taking me through the practice questions on the phone. All I needed was to get 15 questions right to progress to the next stage. I was so grateful he took the time to help me, and thanks to him, I passed.

I rode the feeling of success right into the next interview. It was with KLM Royal Dutch Airlines, one of the most successful airlines in the world. I didn't really believe I was going to get the advertised job as a check-in agent. I considered the interview as another opportunity to practice interview etiquette and to come face-to-face with airline representatives. I thought my chances of landing another job in future might be better if I got to know the people behind the interviews.

I dressed well and got my hair trimmed before strolling into the KLM office. It was in Terminal 4 at Heathrow Airport.

"Nai-lesh Mak-waaa-naaa?" a well-presented Italian man appeared minutes later with a clipboard, scanning the room. He was tall, sharp, and looked like a pilot. He had a friendly face.

"That's me!" I jumped up and followed him down the hallway.

"I am Stefano," he said, leading me to an office down the corridor. "I love your shoes by the way, bellissimo!"

I always appreciated good shoes (I still do).

The interview started and I had never been so blasē - This was interview 36, and there'd likely be plenty more interviews after this.

'So, Nai-lesh, is that how you say your name?'

By then I had developed my little routine to help people pronounce my name correctly. I had stopped calling myself 'Neal.' Your name is an important part of your identity and I found it was better to help people get the pronunciation right than to go for a simplified version. I pointed to my knee.

"No, it's like a 'knee, knee-lesh', Nilesh."

"Ah, I understand! So, Nilesh, why should we consider you?" Stefano said.

"Well, why not?" I chuckled.

Stefano raised his eyebrows and started skimming my resume.

"Mm hmmm... I see you're studying for an aviation degree." – Tick - Stefano moved the pen across his clipboard exuberantly.

"And you passed our test! Perfetto." – Tick.

"You have recent customer service experience from working at Marks & Spencer." - Another tick.

He looked up momentarily and scanned me up and down.

"He dresses well too, with a molto bello haircut," he grinned and held my gaze. It seemed as if Stefano was impressed with me. He turned the page, all that was left were my references. He froze and his jaw dropped.

"Sir Gulam Noon? Like THE Sir Gulam Noon?" he questioned, excitedly.

"The Curry King is your personal reference?"

Not long after I returned to London, my father's friend took me under his wing. He was in London for a few days and was keen to introduce me to some of his business connections.

One of those connections was Sir Gulam Noon, a Mumbai-born, prominent British entrepreneur who had created a number of successful food companies in London. He had earned the title 'Curry King.' He had been awarded a Knighthood by the Queen and was made a Member of the Order of the British Empire.

His business provided chilled and frozen meals to supermarkets and some of Britain's largest airlines including British Airways, Air India, Virgin Atlantic, Jet Airways and Kingfisher.

I had met Sir Noon only briefly, stopping by his offices with my father's friend. He was famous and busy but he still generously gave me his time and said he could put in a good word for me. I have been very fortunate to have an extended network of contacts through family and friends, who have helped to give me a leg-up most international students and migrants aren't as lucky to have. And for that I'm extremely grateful.

But it's okay if you don't have these connections. Don't be afraid to ask for help or reach out to people you normally wouldn't.

"That's very thoughtful of you, Mr Noon, sir. Thank you," I said. "But I really want to find a job myself."

So, instead I accepted his second offer: to list him as a personal reference on my CV, complete with his direct home phone line and email.

Stefano shook his head, "Well Nilesh, I am very impressed," he said.

The rest of the interview was very straightforward. He asked me about my work experience, customer service, why I wanted to work for KLM and how I was planning to juggle a part time job and my studies. After finishing the questions, he said: "Thank you for coming in today, we'll be in touch."

I walked out of the interview thinking nothing of it, making mental notes on how I could answer better the next time. Back to filling out more application forms, I thought on my way home.

This time, however, I was ready to attack those listed job opportunities with more confidence - I passed what I considered to be the hardest obstacle, and that was enough to make me believe that my plane was about to take-off.

A few days later I got the call.

"Nilesh? It's Stefano. KLM would like to formally invite you to two weeks of training, starting Monday. You got the job, bravo!"

I was the first international student from my university to be hired in such a good position during the course of studies. I had got the job against all odds and advice. More than once I had been told flatly that it couldn't be done.

So, when I was given a branded bag, and a three-piece suit complete with shoes, I have to admit I felt pretty smug about myself.

I had to go to Amsterdam to get the uniform fitted, and this was my very first trip outside London. The difference between my uniform and the uniform that pilots wore was hard to notice - just a set of wings on the name badge.

I definitely had my fun with it. Sometimes I would walk into delis, supermarkets or shopping malls, pretending I had come off a long flight. I would tell tall tales about flying to New York or Mexico City – you name it.

One day, I came into my aviation class decked out in KLM attire and sat in the front row, eagerly waiting to see the look on my lecturer's and course coordinator's face.

"Okay class turn to page..." he rushed through the door and stopped when he saw me, his look of surprise transitioning into a smile.

"From now on, you will be known as 'Mr. Catch Me If You Can,'" he said to me after class. It was in reference to the movie starring Leonardo DiCaprio, who successfully poses as a pilot (amongst other things) without any qualifications.

Despite all odds, the boy from India had done it!

I walked into Heathrow Airport for my first official day on the job, reflecting on my initial day in London. I'd come a long way from walking through those arrival gates, jetlagged and haggard, uncertain of what my life would be.

I signed in and walked up to the KLM check-in desks. The queue of passengers had started to form, and I waved my first customer through.

"Have a nice flight," I said, my hand ushering them towards the sign. It read: Welcome to Terminal 4.

Soon it would be my turn to have a nice flight, and over the next few years I would have many.

My Key Takeaways

- Take rejection with a grain of salt: Life is a game of chances. You could secure an opportunity on your first try, or - as was the case with me - it could take more than 350 job applications before your day comes. Trust the process! It's easy for me to say this with hindsight, just know that one day the right opportunity will come.
- Dress smartly for job interviews. Iron your clothes, and if you haven't cut your hair in some time, a trim will do you good. If you don't have a successful outcome, you'll at least feel fresh.
- You may be desperate for a job but don't let the recruiter or the person interviewing you know. Relax and stay cool and go in with an open mind thinking that this will be a fun experience.

Chapter 8

Let The World Be Your Classroom

"I am not the same, having seen the moon shine on the other side of the world."

– Mary Anne Radmacher

There are countless stories out there, just like mine. Stories of rejection and failure.

My favourite is the story of the founder of Alibaba, Jack Ma. He is one of the richest people in the world but there was a time when even Kentucky Fried Chicken wouldn't hire him. There is an incredible story where he is one of 24 applicants in a hiring round and they give everyone a job except him.

Somehow, someway it all just works out.

The second semester went so much better for me than the first, and the next three years of my degree were smooth sailing - or should I say smooth soaring. My practical experience meant I could understand what was taught in class much better.

I had the same approach when I took my A Levels at RIMS. My studies were strengthened when I was running WebT@ntra.

This was the best way for me to study. To blend practical experience and theory. I was now thriving at university. I had fun with friends, I understood my assignments, I saw new countries and cities, and had a great time working at Terminal 4. Don't get me wrong, there were definitely some struggles. I had to spend late nights in the library to meet assignment deadlines and there was always a lot of work to do.

I discovered I was really good at cramming. Before exams I would swap shifts at work and clear my schedule so I could concentrate on my studies for about two weeks. I worked hard and I studied hard, and I loved every second of it.

As a KLM staff member I received airfare discounts and soon I was going to places I'd never heard of before. It was hard to believe my childhood dreams of soaring above the houses of Gujarat had become my reality. I had been given the golden ticket of adventures and you bet I was going to make the most of it.

For the next several years I travelled to places far and near, known and unknown, good and bad. I made the most of any long-weekend or holiday by swapping shifts and going on adventures.

Terminal 4 at Heathrow became the centre of my life. I was living and breathing my studies. It was my school, my classroom.

The people I met along the way were my teachers. My passport? A report card. And I guess that made me a top student. For the first time in my life.

The first of my many trips was to Switzerland, where I was amazed by the picture postcard scenery.

Switzerland (or Swisserland as they say) was just as famous as London in India, mostly due to Bollywood movies. Many had scenes in the Swiss Alps, even if they didn't necessarily fit the plot. They would always show a young couple, madly in love, by a train window, staring deeply into each other's eyes with the green Swiss landscape and majestic snow-capped mountains in the distance.

I always found these films very visually striking. So, I decided to create my own movie scene.

On a train ride through the Swiss countryside, I searched for the cheapest snack on the menu of the pantry cart. I never liked to waste money and I was always on a backpacker's budget, no matter how much I earned. I settled on toast with coffee, which was served with a choice of spreads; small tubs of butter, jams and some kind of chocolate spread.

Wow! The taste exploded in my mouth.

I looked at the packaging. Nutella, where have you been all my life?

"This is amazing!" I beamed up at the waiter, splodges of Nutella most certainly gathered in the corners of my mouth.

"Can I give you the butter back in exchange for some more of these?" I offered the yellow tubs to him with both hands. One of them had a Nutella smear on them.

The waiter snuck me a few more Nutella tubs and some more toast to go with it. The crunchy toast and chocolate were heavenly.

The Swiss countryside was whizzing by as I ate, looking just as romantic and majestic as it did in the movies. I felt like the luckiest guy in the world.

By the way, I would recommend that you carry a jar of Nutella in your backpack. When you are globetrotting, it will come in handy. I have had Nutella spread on crackers, scones, crepes and ciabattas, and I even stuffed it in a pita bread once. My favourite combo was with a freshly baked baguette in France.

It's important to find something simple like that. It can fill you up and light you up at the same time, especially during hard times. Every time I have Nutella now, I am briefly taken back to the Swiss alps.

After I'd made friends in London, it was easy to forget the days when I had felt incredibly lonely and miserably homesick, especially during holidays like Diwali, but I rediscovered the importance of kindness during my travels, particularly one afternoon on an ice rink in Cologne, Germany.

When a German friend I made through university invited me to stay with his family during the Christmas holidays, I said yes straight away. I arrived late in the afternoon. White sprinkles were falling from the sky and a fresh layer of snow was settling over the old city. My friend was not ready to see me yet and I noticed an ice rink nearby. I left the train station to check it out. I had seen movies of people effortlessly gliding around a rink and with some time to kill, I thought I may as well give it a go.

I rented a pair of skates for 20 euros. And then, propelled by both excitement and naiveté (and lots of stupidity) I rushed onto the ice. How hard could it be, right?

It was very hard.

Especially the ice I landed on. Immediately falling onto my backside. Ouch!

For the next 20 minutes, I was either sitting on my bottom or crawling on my hands or knees. I was desperately trying to stand on my feet. I spotted the railing that hugged the rink and made my way towards it, dodging locals as they whooshed by. I kept my legs very still and pulled myself forward by grabbing the railing, slowly making my way round the rink.

At first, I didn't notice the other skaters laughing at me, but I soon realised I had become the entertainment at the rink. I was the only dark-skinned person there and my clothes stood out. Everyone else was wearing sports-wear and bright winter jackets, while I was dressed in jeans and a dark coat.

I felt incredibly self-conscious, and I decided to leave the rink, because I knew I looked ridiculous. It also stung that no one offered to help. Some people never evolve beyond high school and sometimes it never occurs to people that you might be an outsider, trying to immerse yourself in their culture. Trying to learn something they could do as easily and naturally as walking and talking is to others.

But as I carefully dragged myself to the exit of the ice rink, I met a couple of German people who knew the value of kindness.

They caught me as I was about to fall again.

"Do you need help?" a woman smiled.

A German man skated up beside us and asked me where I was from. The ice was broken.

"I am from London, and this is my first-time skating," I squeaked.

I was a little overwhelmed with emotion, I had been at breaking point and these strangers had come to rescue me.

"Keine sorge," said the woman on my right. "Don't worry."

"We'll teach you! Just move your legs, that's it - right foot, left foot, and right foot again. Now push your feet out to the sides, there you go..."

This is how it continued for the next hour or so. The two women pulled me along as the man skated behind, ready to catch me just in case. I had been having a terrible nightmare just moments earlier, but this kindness from strangers had turned the experience into a wonderful dream and I closed my eyes, feeling the snow land on my face as I slowly glided around and around.

The laughter had stopped, those watching from outside the rink silent as they contemplated what this idiot (me) was up to now.

When they let go of my arms, I imagined I looked something like a baby deer or horse trying to stand for the first time - all limbs and no grace. But I was doing it! I was skating on my own.

My new friends cheered. After two hours on the rink, I had had enough and swapped the skates for my shoes.

I wanted to thank this trio, so I bought them hot chocolate. We had a nice chat, and they practiced their English on me. It was an experience I would never forget.

I had skated on ice, and it was all thanks to their kindness.

With KLM, the perks didn't just stop at discounted airfare - if you didn't call in sick for a whole year, you were given two free plane tickets.

Halima, another friend from university, suggested maximising my well-earned trip by picking the longest route - an 11-12-hour flight to Japan. She wanted to come too, and she offered to pay for our accommodation if I gave her my second ticket. I was in the middle of writing my honours thesis. It was a 10,000-word document on how the Airbus A380 has impacted airlines and airports. It was a challenging topic, and I knew the long flight would give me time to work on it without interruptions. I often used my travels as study time and rather enjoyed these opportunities to hunker down and get some work in.

Luckily, both of us got upgraded to business class when we boarded the flight. This smoothed things over for us, as we'd had a little tiff while waiting in the boarding queue. She didn't want to go about our Japan trip in the random way I usually did. She needed plans and schedules. When we landed, we decided we would go separate ways and fill our days the way we wanted to. We'd rather have a good time on our own, meet back at the airport and share our adventures flying back, than risk our friendship. Some people don't travel well together, and that's fine.

I only had two things on my agenda in Japan: to see the first blossoming flower of spring, the ume (plum) blossoms at the Yushima Tenjin shrine and to visit Susuma - the first person I had met when I landed in London. Once again there he was, waiting for me at the arrivals gate, a big smile on his face, just this time in Tokyo.

We headed straight to a restaurant, and it became clear very early on that Japan was like no other place I had ever been to before. It was the most interesting country, but also the most bizarre.

We scanned the menu, which was displayed on iPads. That's not new or considered very high tech now but this was the mid-2000s, so it was pretty ground-breaking. Something wasn't quite right about this restaurant, and I just couldn't put my finger on it. Then it hit me, there was no staff to wait on us!

We ordered via the iPad and our meals appeared on trays through a hatch in front of the table shortly after. Minimal human interaction. I thought back to the time I had my Marks & Spencer interview, arranging the coffee and sugar neatly on the tray and how my presentation - and customer care - had ultimately landed me the job.

If there had been one of these restaurants back in London, well, I may never have got the job and my life would have panned out very differently. There are just some things automations can't replace -

service with a smile is one of them. Susuma and I settled in with our meals, chatting away.

"Can you believe it Nilesh, four years ago we met in London and here we are," Susuma said grinning.

"Yes, on February 6th all those years ago!" I replied, trying to manoeuvre my chopsticks correctly.

Susuma's face lit up.

"What is it?" I asked, my noodles slipping through the chopsticks back into my bowl. "Today, today is February 6th!" he said excitedly.

It was a bizarre coincidence, and totally unplanned, that Susuma would happen to pick me up from the airport once more on the exact same day four years later.

Sometimes life is funny like that.

But it wasn't the only bizarre thing to happen to me that day.

Japan is very high tech, not just with their automated ordering in restaurants, but in bathrooms, too. The toilets were not like normal toilets. The seat was a cushion, and you could control the temperature. One button said 'flush' but when I pressed it, only the sound of flushing could be heard. There were different 'shower' settings that made water spurt out like a fountain within the toilet bowl. And the actual flush button? Well, it was where you'd normally expect it.

"Susuma, why would a toilet have a button for a flushing sound, but no flush?" I asked, really confused.

"Oh yes, yes... well, that's for when you do a... number 2," he giggled.

"What?" things were getting more bizarre by the second.

"Japanese, we're very polite you see, we don't like anyone listening in."

Susuma was right - the Japanese were incredibly polite, even the people in authority.

Tokyo was a truly beautiful place, where nature and constructions blended into each other. Spring flowers neatly climbed up walls, and trees stood intertwined. The flower beds were so well organised, and structured in the most amazing compositions and designs, but I never saw a gardener maintaining them. I wondered how on earth they trained these flowers and plants to be so well-behaved.

I enjoyed visiting the Starbucks at Shibuya Crossing - the busiest intersection in the world, made famous through many movies. The coffee was quite expensive, so I'd just get hot water from the barista and help myself to the free chocolate powder and milk at the drink station instead. I would sit and watch the crowds of people outside the window. Traffic would stop and hundreds and hundreds of people would descend on the crossing. I'd wonder where everyone was busily heading off too.

Lost in looking at the crowds moving in waves across the road I thought about Gujarat and the cows that would stop traffic in my hometown. I felt a pang of homesickness but also gratitude for the life I had. I collected myself and hit the 'send' button, submitting my thesis. My university days were officially over, and I had marked the occasion sitting at a coffee shop on the other side of the world.

When the day came for the graduation ceremony of the 'Class of 2010' at the University of West London, I pictured scenes similar to those in the movies - fireworks and throwing our hats in the air. As any student can appreciate, graduation ceremonies are expensive! There's hat and gown hire, professional photos and for international students, the additional cost of accommodating your family from afar. It was too expensive for my family to fly so I graduated alongside my London family - my fellow student friends. I thought

I would feel changed somehow post-graduation. That there would be a feeling of pure euphoria. But after hours waiting for my name to be called for 5 seconds of stage time, a handshake, and the handing over of a certificate, it was a bit anticlimactic.

We didn't toss our hats into the sky. Fireworks did not explode above out heads.

My expectations of the graduation ceremony were far from reality.

My expectations of travel on the other hand, well, they surpassed all my wildest dreams.

My Key Takeaways

- There is more to the university experience than just hitting the books - take the opportunity to truly live the student life, join committees, go to parties, make lifelong friends, and expand your social circles: look for opportunities to make friends beyond people from within your culture, so you don't get stuck in your own 'little India'.
- Find a job in the industry aligned to what you are studying, or as close to it as you can get. This will not only help you understand your lectures and topics better, but you will also be able to create a network of people in the same industry you want a career in, and it will be easier for you to land a job after you graduate. The biggest mistake students make, international as well as local, is to take crummy part time jobs instead of finding something more relevant, thinking that they are not ready for the industry or that they don't know enough to apply for a good job.
- I never saw myself as a student. I would dress and behave like a professional at university, as well as outside the university walls. Sometimes people would mistake me for a lecturer, rather than a student, but by not adopting the student attitude I was able to achieve more during my studies and get real industry experience as I did not appear as a student, who would be inexperienced and immature.

Chapter 9

Diversity

"Knowledge will give you power, but character respect."

– Bruce Lee

Each time I travelled and had these amazing experiences, I would return to Terminal 4 with a renewed appreciation for people and culture and food - but most of all, for differences and similarities.

The more I saw of the world, the more my mind welcomed new ideas and I contemplated the real meaning and ramifications of 'inherited diversity' and 'acquired diversity'.

As I mentioned earlier, in parts of India, many people believe disability is punishment for misbehaviour in a previous life - that you have bad karma and deserve whatever limitations you have. This view is changing, and I think we can thank globalisation for this. The more people travel and see the differences and similarities between people with their own eyes, the better they understand each other and develop empathy.

Popular culture also plays an important role in educating us.

Unfortunately, Indian cinema has a history of reinforcing social stigmas and making characters with physical disabilities and mental health conditions the butt of jokes. Things are changing now. Children can learn the value of diversity by watching a lot of good shows on television. But for me, travelling and experiencing life outside my hometown opened my eyes to the beauty of being different and the many other ways in which people can live their lives.

So, I would travel with my eyes wide open, a jar of Nutella and often a book, or more specifically, Robin Sharma's, The Monk Who Sold His Ferrari.

It's a great book – one of my favourites – the title would often catch someone's eye when I was reading it on the plane and I was always happy to strike up a conversation.

Meeting new and interesting people is part of the fun that naturally comes with travelling, so don't be afraid to say hello or start a conversation with strangers, if they seem interested. You never know who you might bump into.

Sometimes, as a KLM staff member, I would get an upgrade to business class. It was very luxurious, and I loved every minute of it, and it was much easier to strike up a conversation with someone when travelling. This was true even in economy as you were practically sitting on top of each other anyway.

While travelling to Brazil for the first time, the man seated next to me happened to be an incredibly prolific surgeon, known for his work with Michael Jackson, and we got chatting after he inquired about my book.

I told him about my love of Nutella and my home country, and he told me about his yacht, which was moored in Rio de Janeiro's revered Guanabara Bay. It sits below Sugarloaf Mountain, where the famous statue of Christ the Redeemer (Cristo Redentor) stands. Once the plane landed, he asked me if I'd like to visit him at the yacht club, so he could introduce me to what he believed I would love just as much as Nutella, if not more - something called acai.

What did I have to lose?

Nothing could possibly be better than Nutella, of course, but spending a day at a private yacht club sounded extravagant and exciting.

We exchanged details and arranged to meet within the next few days. I was lucky to meet Taj while working at KLM, a Brazilian colleague who had organised for me to stay with his family in Rio. I was surprised by how much Indian culture I saw. At that time Brazil was rather enchanted by India, thanks to a popular television soap opera. The country embraced my homeland and I saw saris and kurtas for sale at flea markets, lots of India-inspired yoga classes and more.

The yacht club near Sugarloaf Mountain was lavish. It had sweeping views of the bay and hilly terrain. The statue of Christ the Redeemer was just visible on the peak of the mountain. Typically, when Indians are travelling, we tend to stick to our own circles and food. I think we all find it easier to stick to what we know, but you should always consider what you might be missing out on. The world is a delightful buffet.

Two bowls arrived at our table, full of a thick, bright purple pulp.

The surgeon told me it was acai, a berry native to rainforests and incredibly rich in antioxidants. It was frozen and made into a thick smoothie topped with granola, bananas and cream. I dipped my spoon in and it was love at first bite.

"Aaaaaaah-çaaai," I sighed. It was such a very refreshing, cold treat.

Since then, I have attempted to recreate my own version of acai bowls for breakfast (or even a cool lunch on a hot summer day).

Like my first date with Nutella, I just couldn't get enough of acai.

The surgeon was returning home the next day, so I asked him where I could get acai and a view like this again. He made a deal with the yacht club's chairman and told me I could continue to visit the club under his name and eat all the acai I wanted for the rest of my stay in Rio. I couldn't believe my luck!

Every morning I took in breath-taking views, basked in the sunshine and ate my fill of purple berries.

I thanked Hanuman - surely this was his doing, or the work of some other gods. Maybe it was karma, although I couldn't quite recall what good deed I had done to deserve this.

Or maybe, it was all because I had a good book.

I was sleeping under the stars in a desert somewhere in Kenya, thinking of how many times I'd lain in the open just like this, as a kid on the roof of my home in Rajkot.

Travelling the world taught me more history and geography than I'd ever learnt at school. It made my dreams come true. I was flying as I always wanted to as a child.

There is much to learn and many interesting people to meet, even on planes. So the next time you stick your nose in a book or watch an inflight movie, just remember the stranger sitting next to you could be a lot more entertaining.

I didn't need an impressive book to get chatting to a friendly couple en route to Romania. The gentleman, who had an impressive moustache, was from a south eastern European country and his wife was Dutch. They were both quite tall people, and I was sitting in the aisle seat next to them. I broke the ice by asking if I could sit by the window, and they introduced themselves as Toni and Stijnie. They told me they lived in a small town near Amsterdam and were on their way to visit family in Romania.

I was planning to go to Bucharest, and then to Constanta, a seaside town in the south of the country. I hadn't figured out how I was going to get from the airport to this town, a few hours away, but as luck would have it, Stijnie and Toni were heading to the same place. Even more coincidental was the fact that my accommodation was right next door to where Toni's sister lived. It was too good to be true - it had so easily fallen into place, just by simply saying 'hi' on a plane.

So off we went in a private car, the next few hours solidifying what would become a long-standing friendship. From then on, any time I travelled I would meet Stijnie and Toni on my Amsterdam layovers. KLM's main airport is Schiphol in the Netherland's capital, which meant I saw them often.

If we had time, they would pick me up and take me to their home where they'd offer a spread of amazing breads, cheeses and coffee. I shared my adventures with them, and they told me about their own travels. They gave me advice and fussed over me, they were fantastic friends. They became the Dutch version of Maneck Aunty and Phiroze Uncle.

On one occasion they also came to stay with me in London for a week. If the world was my classroom, they were my teachers, checking in to make sure I'd done my 'homework' on my next destination.

I am usually up for a challenge, and I love to share my worldview with others.

One day while visiting the beautiful French city Nice, my Brazilian friend Jacqui and I had a conversation about money. I told her I didn't think money was the secret to a wonderful life. Jacqui disagreed.

"I don't believe you Nilesh," Jacqui said over breakfast, "Money is everything, money is happiness, you can't do anything without money."

"You can still have a great time without money too," I said, "I'll prove it to you - let's try and go an entire day without spending any money!"

It happened to be the day we planned to take a bus to Monte Carlo, one of the casino capitals of the world. It was going to be a little harder than I thought, but we managed to get ourselves a spot on the double decker bus without a ticket, a good start to our money-free day. It wasn't very ethical. I do not encourage sneaking in the middle door on public transport by hiding behind the people who were getting off. You can get fined heavily. But we did it for the sake of the experiment – and were very lucky it worked.

The first stop was Le Palais des Princes De Monaco, set on top of a cliff overlooking multi-million-dollar yachts. I saw Jacqui's face fall when she saw the entry price. There was a large group of tourists climbing on board a bus and I had an idea. I asked her to just stick with me as I ran up to one of the guards.

"Sir! We have left our camera inside! May we please go grab it? We were part of the tour that came out just now and the bus is leaving in ten minutes!" I pointed to the bus and waved at the driver, pretending that we had some kind of agreement where he would wait for us. The driver waved back with a quizzical look on his face.

The guard let us in without question and without checking to see if we had paid an entry fee. The gardens were beautiful, and we took our time wandering around the palace. There was an ice cream shop right near the exit, with a 'free taste tests' sign. We walked in and tried ten different types of ice cream. A great morning snack. We headed down the hill to the river, where there was a ferry. It was part of a Monte Carlo tour pass and it went straight from the palace to the casino.

I spoke to the driver, "Sir! We left our bag in the taxi that had our tickets, what should we do now?"

He told us to hop right on board. The ferry ride, though short, was incredibly beautiful and I felt as if I was in a scene from a movie. The wind was rushing through my hair, and Monte Carlo's world-famous casino was just visible in the distance. And it was made all the more beautiful because it was free. But trouble struck when Jacqui insisted we go inside.

"Nilesh! It's Monte Carlo, we have to!" she pleaded.

To enter, you had to make a 25 euro bet. I told her I don't gamble, and I don't drink alcohol, they were my key life rules.

She ended up paying for both of us, which put a dent in our experiment. She wanted to play roulette. All I knew about the game was that you had to choose between red or black. I suggested red. And sure enough, on the first play, Jacqui lost 25 euros. Then she bet on black and won it back. She placed it on red again and won another 25 euros. Jacqui wanted to keep going, but I asked her to slow down. She had already recovered her initial losses and I could still prove that you didn't need money to have a good time. I reminded her of the phrase 'quit while you're ahead.'

"Let's quit now while we're up, we'll have enough for lunch."

While we were eating our sandwiches, a parade of dancers circled around the restaurant. They were promoting some sort of dance club, Sea Lounge, down by the water. We started chatting with one of the guys who was part of the parade, who happened to be Brazilian, like Jacqui. He was the DJ at the club.

"Why don't you guys come down as my guests tonight, free entry at the door, bottle of champagne on me," he smiled.

What luck. Later that night, we were escorted to a booth where we joined two other women - one from Belgium and the other from Sweden - who were also on the DJ's special guest list. We had the best night dancing and laughing in this prestigious club filled with persons whom I assumed were well-known or wealthy Europeans. The women particularly enjoyed the bottle of champagne they had all to themselves, while I stuck to my H2O on the rocks. We left the club after midnight, when the buses had stopped. Hoping for the best, we stuck our thumbs out. Not long after a French man, who appeared to be dressed in boxing gear, pulled over.

"Heading to Nice?" he said, winding down the window. We nodded. "Allons! Come on!"

The women piled into the back and I took the front seat and off we went.

He was a fighter of some sort and had just finished a match, he explained in a heavy French accent. We got back to Nice at 2 am and found a kebab shop that had yet to call it a night. Our new friends treated Jacqui and I to kebabs. As we sat on the Nice foreshore, I realised I had made my point. Besides the little splurge at the casino - which Jacqui won back and more - we had gone a whole day without spending a cent.

We finished our adventure with some skinny dipping and then headed back to our accommodation.

Before we went to bed, Jacqui was reminded of our experience. She turned to me.

"You're right," she said smiling, "You can have so much fun without spending any money! But I still think you need money to be happy. Without winning in roulette, we wouldn't have eaten proper food all day, just sampled ice cream."

I guess this meant we were both partly right.

Like the cows of Gujarat, I was a free agent, an explorer who always somehow found a friend or a home I could turn to.

All these friends I made during my travels meant I had places to stay when my plane touched down. It meant I had a local tour guide who could explain how best to navigate a destination and best of all, it meant I was never truly alone.

I am still in touch with many of the new friends I met along the way - Romanian, Canadian, Brazilian, Chinese, American, and more – so many years later. Some even came all the way to India to celebrate my wedding. But I had to talk my way out of a Mexican holding cell before that happened.

My Key Takeaways

- Travelling is the best education money can buy.
- Always keep your family in the loop when it comes to your flight itinerary and research embassy locations, you never know when

you might need it! Sometimes I'd travel somewhere without knowing where I would sleep but I would always make sure that my sister or brother knew where I was in the world and send them details about the closest embassy or consulate.

- Make as many new friends as you can – and try and keep in touch with them. In today's world it is so easy.
- Travelling by yourself can be a lot of fun – never hesitate to go anywhere just because you don't have company.

Chapter 10

The Power Of Language

"Do you know what a foreign accent is? It's a sign of bravery."

– Amy Chua

I learned the hard way that communication really is the key in many situations. In business, in customer service, relationships, marriage and most of all, while being detained during one of my travels.

I was in Mexico, very nervous, in a small and boiling hot cell.

I could hear a couple of officers speaking Spanish in the next room as I sat waiting, wondering if the sweat dripping down my face was a result of the Mexican heat or pure panic. I managed to communicate with non-English speaking people all over the world using limited words and exaggerated body language. But it didn't work this time. I was feeling completely lost and frustrated. I didn't understand what was happening and my happy-go-lucky attitude had evaporated. I was in some kind of trouble with the authorities.

I had arrived at Mexico City airport from Amsterdam some hours ago, only to be whisked away by men in uniform who wanted to ask me questions. I was soon placed in a hot glass box with people from many other countries. There were Romanians, Iranians, and a couple of Indians, too. I longed for my jar of Nutella, but it was in my backpack and that had been taken from me.

I didn't have any other luggage. I always travelled light - it was easier to get around that way. Just a couple of shirts, jeans, a few toiletries, some space for souvenirs and of course, Nutella and a book.

While I was waiting, a border security officer visited the room to ask a pair of Romanians some questions.

"Where are you from? Where are you going? How much money do you have?"

I started to get a little worried - why was I here? I had just come for a holiday. Nothing suspicious. When would it be my turn to answer questions?

Many of my newfound 'cell mates' had come and gone while I was waiting. I was hungry, nervous, a little scared and worried about what might happen to me. Luckily, the officers had not taken my mobile phone. I typed out a text message, very discreetly, while casually chatting to the person sitting next to me.

"If you do not hear from me within 2 hours, call the Indian Embassy in Mexico City. I am being detained at the airport," I wrote to my brother in Mumbai. I put my hand in my jacket pocket, holding the unlocked phone, ready to press 'Send.'

A possible reason for my detention dawned on me. I had come from Amsterdam, which was both the headquarters for KLM and one of the world's largest drug consumers.

And I had travelled to Mexico City – a place with a reputation for producing a lot of narcotics. My mind started racing in that little cell. What were these border security agents thinking? Did they believe I was a drug mule for a cartel? My imagination certainly got the better of me and I was getting increasingly worried.

An officer entered the room and stood in front of me, oozing authority. I did not know what to expect but I thought of the worst.

"You've got it all wrong!" I was about to shout.

But the officer broke the silence before I could say anything.

"Sir, you're free to go," he said, handing me my passport.

I was relieved, but also felt annoyed.

Any sensible person would have gritted their teeth, forced a smile, and got out of there as fast as their legs could carry them. But not me.

"Excuse me, sir, can I ask why you have held me here for so long?" I asked, folding my arms and standing firm.

"Well, you have no equipaje, no check in luggage, just a backpack" he said, in broken English. "And your passport looked suspicious."

"Oh," I said, taking all this in, looking at my shabby, well-travelled passport. It was held together by a rubber band and did look a little dodgy, especially because of the ink stain soaked through it. An accident due to the Indian Consulate in London, actually.

"We also share a border here with los gringos, Americans, you see," he said, "Many people come here to try to gain an easy way into the US. But we saw you had travelled to many places, and you already have a 10-year US visa anyway."

"I am just here for a holiday," I said, unfolding my arms. "I never got a chance to tell you."

"Si, but you are free to go now," he said.

He moved me out of the room and waved me goodbye. He was ready to get on with the rest of his day – perhaps looking to catch a real drug mule.

The officer handed me over to his colleague in immigration and wished me a good time in Mexico. Another stamp for my collection

- I was slowly making my way around the world, one city at a time. It was an accomplishment for any Indian, considering the process one needed to go through to get approval to travel in the first place. I walked out of the arrival gates and headed for the information desk. I was frugal at the best of times, but more so when I travelled. I packed light and I spent light too. I wanted to avoid costly fares as much as possible.

"Hola, taxi?" the information desk man asked.

"Hola! No. Bus? Train?" I said. I pointed out the location of the hostel I was staying at on my map.

"Not safe for you, not safe for tourists," he said, shaking his head dismissively.

"I don't want to spend money on a taxi," I insisted.

I was working out the conversions in my head. US dollars to Pounds and Pounds to the Indian Rupee. I did not want to spend the money if I could avoid it.

It was getting dark outside and after the day I'd had, I just wanted dinner and bed. A man with long hair, whose familiarity I couldn't quite place, came up beside me and touched my arm.

"Where are you heading, mi amigo?" he asked. I studied his face. Where had I seen him before, a movie possibly?

"To this hostel," I said pointing to my map again. Maybe it was an advertisement in the inflight magazine, maybe that's where I had seen his face. He did look like the model type.

"I can take you, I live near there," he said, tucking his long hair behind his ear. His face was too familiar, too ingrained in my mind for me to have only seen it fleetingly in a magazine. I paused; do

I trust a stranger? If public transport here was considered dangerous, then what about a stranger's car? A stranger's car without the comfort of a taxi licence.

"Are you sure?" I asked. Then it dawned on me: Yes! That was it. I finally figured it out. He was the spitting image of Jesus Christ, with his shoulder length hair and slightly tanned skin. He was even wearing a cross around his neck, and a white pullover shirt with an open neck.

"Of course, mi amigo, no hay problema, it's on my way. I'm here to pick up my aunt and take her home. My name's Hah-zoos," he said, extending his hand for me to shake.

"Hah-zoos? Nice to meet you, I'm Nilesh," I shook his hand.

"Hola, taxi?" the information man asked.

"El viaja con cositas. El equipaje, es caro?" he asked, it sounded like something one of the officers had said earlier.

"Sorry I don't speak Spanish," I shrugged.

"You travel light," he said, translating, "luggage, it's expensive?"

"No, I just travel light," I replied.

We started chatting – it turned out Hahzoos was actually a taxi driver after all. He had knocked off a few hours earlier but had returned to pick up his aunt who was flying in from California. I felt a little more at ease.

His taxi identification card was hanging from his pocket and I squinted to make out the company name and serial number. I wanted to feel safe and give my family as much information as possible in case Hahzoos was not as kind as he seemed.

I texted my family to let them know I had been released from the holding cell and was ready to start my Mexican adventure. I furrowed my brows as I tried to make sense of the tiny letters....surely not. I reread the card over and over. No, my eyes weren't playing tricks on me, his name: Jesus! To make things even weirder, his aunt was named Mary and she was a nun - what were the chances!

"Your name is Jesus?" I asked. I couldn't believe it.

"No, Hah-zoos," he said.

"But it says Jesus, right there!" I pointed.

"Pronunciation, mi amigo," he said, understanding the source of my confusion. "In Spanish we don't say 'jay' we say' hah,' like Ha-maica."

"Jamaica?"

"Hah-maica, si."

I had found a modern-day Jesus, and he had truly been my saviour.

The day had been a rollercoaster of emotions. I was worried that the Mexican Government was going to jail me for trafficking drugs. I was worried border agents were going to decide I was a stowaway looking for a new life in America and deport me. And I was more than a little concerned that I was going to be kidnapped. But I was ending it with Jesus and surely that was a good sign.

As he was driving me home, I was thinking through the life lessons I had learned since I had arrived in Mexico.

Firstly, keep your passport in good condition. Secondly, learn the language of the country you are visiting – even just enough to hold a conversation with the authorities and taxi drivers. And thirdly, if you're ever detained at an airport – especially if the room is sweltering – don't be afraid to ask for a glass of water!

There's an English saying - 'actions speak louder than words' - that many believe is true. But I don't know if that's always the case. You decide after reading about the following incident

Remember Sanjay bhai, the man I met on my first day in London? The Indian from the corner shop, who had sold me the international calling card? Well, we kept in touch over the years and he later started a side business - self-catered apartments in Dubai. They were by the water at Jumeirah Beach and he planned to rent them to business people. This was before Airbnb and it looked like a promising idea,

He knew my background in website development and asked me to help him execute a marketing plan. He was planning a trip to Dubai with his family and offered that I should tag along.

How could I say no?

The Burj Al Arab hotel was at the top of my list to visit in Dubai – it was one of the first seven-star luxury hotels in the world. But at upwards of 11,000 pounds per night, staying there was certainly not an option - I'm no Maharaja! The only way you could visit the hotel was if you had a booking, but that also included dining. Breakfast was the cheapest meal at 170 pounds per person.

I was earning well enough at that time, and thinking it would be a once in a life time experience, I booked breakfast for two.

I didn't want to go alone and thankfully Sanjay's wife Jyoti, who had also never been, was all too happy to accompany me.

We arrived at the big security gates and there it was, like a majestic sailing ship, standing tall against the mass of the tropical blue ocean. I had died and arrived in royalty heaven. Once our ID was checked and our booking confirmed we were escorted to our very own chauffeur driven Rolls Royce.

As we drove over the bridge to the hotel entrance, we were dazzled by an impressive display of water and fire. It felt as if we were arriving at a Sultan's palace. We had dressed as smartly as we could, but we still felt that we didn't look as polished as we should have.

Bright colours and gold fittings caught my eye everywhere I turned. We walked through the lobby. I don't think there is any Indian or English word that can truly capture the magnificence of the Burj Al Arab.

We were greeted as Mr. and Mrs. Makwana, but neither of us bothered to correct them. While it was harmless taking my friend's wife to breakfast, it would probably have seemed a little strange to persons who have grown up in Dubai. We decided to play along.

We were escorted to breakfast, which was downstairs in the hotel's aquarium restaurant where the colours of coral glistened with the movement of water. It was clear no expense had been spared in developing this hotel. We strolled to our table and did our very best to look as if we belonged. They had a buffet, and there were so many delicacies to choose from - pastries, fresh fruits and every condiment you could possibly think of and more. My mouth was watering at every table. The choices were endless.

Burj Al Arab felt like utopia. It seemed as if I had stepped into a perfect world, where my every whim was addressed with enthusiasm. Every staff member we passed greeted us by name. I'm still not sure how they even knew it.

"What would you like to start with Mr. and Mrs. Makwana?" a waiter said as he bowed.

Jyoti and I exchanged a sly smile across the table.

I was feeling slightly overwhelmed with all the choices. I had no idea...

"Perhaps you don't know where to start?" he enquired. That was freaky - had he read my mind? I had read blogs from guests saying the staff was so attentive it was as if they were in your head.

"I am happy to gather some things for you to try, Mr. and Mrs. Makwana?" he asked with a bright, warm smile.

Moments later a beautiful cup was placed in front of me, the bright red bits of strawberry beckoning my taste buds. It was the most amazing jam I had ever tasted in my life. I no longer cared about trying anything else, I just wanted more of this miracle spread. I grabbed crisp slices of toasted sourdough bread and small, crunchy oat biscuits. Anything I could spread the jam on.

Many will say that for 170 pounds, I should have had more than jam. But I don't regret it – trust me, it tasted like magic.

After breakfast we ventured upstairs to explore the rest of the 'palace'. We strolled through a few luxury designer stores and walked past hundreds of fresh flowers placed around the hotel. Eventually, we stumbled on the high-tea area. There was a large sign, in a collection of languages, printed in gold-coloured lettering - I wouldn't have been surprised at all if it was real gold.

NO PHOTOS • 写真か ゛ない • ***Pas de photos***
• ***Keine Fotos*** • 没有照片 •روصدجوتال

We wanted to take a photo anyway. It was a once-in-a-lifetime opportunity and Jyoti and I wanted to preserve a memory of it.

We decided to do it quickly and avoid any trouble, but we were spotted before we could take the picture. Even when guests are breaking a rule, the Burj Al Arab staff handle it politely and happily.

"Mr. and Mrs. Makwana, please, let me take this for you," a man came rushing over with a smile, hand outstretched.

"If you just follow me over here, I can take a photo of you both in front of this nice 24-carat gold pillar."

Before I had a chance to object, we were being ushered politely over to a nearby gold pillar. I smiled for the photo. I didn't have a chance to suggest we go back to the tearoom. The man quickly moved us along.

"Follow me, I know just the spot with a wonderful background I'm sure Mrs. Makwana will love, right next to our beautiful fountain."

We were courteously guided further away from the high-tea area, back down the stairs to the main lobby, where, after taking many more 'couple' photos, we were finally left alone. I was feeling just a tad befuddled but he had certainly taken some great photos. We wanted to explore more, so we decided to take a sneak peek of the Sky Lounge Restaurant. We hopped into a clear glass lift that revealed stunning panoramas of Dubai the higher we climbed. But when we got to the top, a staff member was waiting for us.

"Hello Mr. and Mrs. Makwana, I trust you are enjoying your time with us and hope you were pleased with your breakfast. Unfortunately, the Sky Lounge is closed," she said attentively.

Again, how on earth did all these people know my name?

"Do you wish me to check the available bookings for you this evening?" she offered, her eyes darting to my camera.

"Oh, that's okay we have other dinner reservations tonight," I improvised. All I wanted to do was to take a photo from the top of the building.

"Sir, if you go back in this lift, you can take many mesmerising photos of the sea on your way down," she said, pressing the elevator button.

When we got back to the ground floor, we figured there wasn't much else we could do or see without a restaurant reservation. I took one last look at the opulent lobby before we made our way to the exit. We were handed a survey card.

Most of it was what you'd expect. They wanted feedback on the meal and overall experience. But the last question caught my eye.

During your stay here with us, did any of our staff use the word 'no'?

No - no they didn't.

Despite my best efforts to go exploring where I shouldn't, not once did any staff member show annoyance, anger or disapproval. They just politely redirected me and phrased their rejections carefully, as if they genuinely wanted to help. It was brilliant customer service. Here, at one of the most expensive hotels in the world, I learnt the power of not saying 'no.'

Sure, I was no Maharaja, but that day I certainly felt like I was. It had all come down to the purposeful choice of language. Actions speak louder than words, you say? Not always.

Although the novelty of exploring the world and travelling to a new city every couple of weeks had yet to wear off, no matter what map I picked up, I couldn't shake this feeling of being adrift. In London's Underground one day after finishing another shift at KLM, I bumped into Mahatma Gandhi. Right in the tube network. His face was plastered on a poster. I grew up with his likeness featured on Indian currency, so I was taken aback to see it on the walls of a train in a foreign country.

I knew he was considered the Father of the Nation in India. He freed us from the British Empire in 1948. I had some basic information, but I was yet to truly understand who Gandhi was and why he inspired so many people.

One thing that always baffled me when travelling around the world, was how much everyone knew about Gandhi. People were always talking about him. When they met me, they would ask about him. People abroad knew more about Gandhi than I did, even though I had done projects on him in school and read books about him.

I had seen statues of him all over the world. I had even stumbled across a few nonviolent protests in his name.

I looked at the poster.

"There's more to life than increasing its speed" - M. K. Gandhi.

What did this mean? I stood there spellbound for a few moments just staring at it.

I left the train still thinking about it. I headed home wondering what he meant. I had hardly been in my London apartment in weeks. My foot was firmly on the accelerator pedal ever since I'd moved to London, and even more so since I had graduated. I was certainly enjoying the journey, but I hadn't stopped to pause and reflect on the destination.

Where was I actually heading? Maybe there was more to life than always living in the fast lane. I'd spent six years in London, half the time as a student and the other half working. I felt it was time for a change. I had enjoyed my time in aviation. It had helped me to achieve my dreams of flying. But I had an entrepreneurial streak in me that I hadn't explored in years. It was starting to pull me in another direction. Geographically, spiritually – I wanted change. My subconscious had a destination in mind that I didn't know about yet. But I was about to find it.

My Key Takeaways

- Language is powerful: words can indicate a sense of respect, can change your experience, or make you think differently about something. Take the time to learn some common phrases of the local language.
- Some experiences require money. While money can be earned again, opportunities to certain experiences may not present themselves ever again. I'm not saying to skip paying your rent to go bungee jumping, but if you're able to tighten your food budget for a few weeks in order to enjoy 170 pound jam in an extraordinary place, I say go for it.

Chapter 11

No

"Life keeps throwing me curve balls and I don't even own a bat. At least my dodging skills are improving."

– Jayleigh Cape

After visiting Rio, it was hard to shake the desire to lie in the sun. I returned to London's wet and cold weather and began dreaming of a sunburnt country. It was time to leave. I decided to move to Brazil.

I had been there twice now and I was somewhat of a novelty there, like western people were in India. I admit I enjoyed the attention, but I also saw a business opportunity; Brazilians were very interested in Indian culture and it sparked a business idea. Perhaps it was time for me to be my own boss again, to let the businessman in me take the steering wheel and control the speed at which my life was moving.

WebT@ntra had been plodding along by my side ever since I left India, and I had juggled my KLM job, studies and delivering web projects.

Now I felt a need to move on and set my new plan in motion. I booked the domain braziltoindia.com. I wanted to start a business that provided guided tours from Brazil to India.

Remember my friend who was running a travel company back in Mumbai and had let me use his office for some time? We agreed he could take care of the business from the travel perspective, while I could do what I did best from Brazil - meet people and sell the service.

Most Brazilians had London, Paris and New York at the top of their bucket lists, but they had gained a new appetite for the Far East. Everything Indian, including clothing, culture, religion and Bollywood movies, was now trendy, and tourism from Brazil to India was rapidly picking up.

I was excited to be my own boss again and looked forward to many more acai bowls, in the yacht club - who knew, my surgeon friend could even be my first customer!

Just a few weeks later I gave away all the possessions in my London flat.

I did not want to keep much and only packed my favourite clothes and shoes. I let go of everything else.

Need a desk?

Take mine!

Need a TV?

Here, this is yours.

I resigned from KLM and invited my friends and colleagues to a farewell party. Everyone was baffled, it had all happened very quickly!

With a brand-new business card in my pocket, I jumped onto a flight to Mumbai. I thought I'd stay with my family for a few weeks, while setting up the new business. I was excited to start afresh, own a business and move to Brazil. Everything was falling into place perfectly.

Until I told my father about my plans.

He had mostly been supportive, sometimes surprisingly supportive, of my crazy plans my whole life. But at this point, he couldn't have been less enthused.

He didn't want me to move to Brazil. He wanted me to get married. I was his youngest child and without a life partner. Family life is highly valued in India. I knew that I was going to face pressure when I returned and that explaining my ambitions and adventures was unlikely to sway the opinion of my family. They would want to know when I was going to meet a nice Indian woman and settle down, especially my father. "I am putting my foot down," he said over dinner the night I told him about my Brazil plans. "No. There is no way I am letting you move to a country full of drugs and kidnapping, it's not safe there!"

I looked quizzically over to my sister. Why did he think this about Brazil?

She told me there had been a documentary on TV just two weeks ago, focused on Brazilian favelas, gangs, cartels and organised crime. It was just my luck.

"Really, it's not safe anywhere!" I said.

"Take your rose-tinted glasses off, beta and open your eyes," he said. "No son of mine will be moving to that country, anywhere but there. You are not moving to Brazil and I'm not going to repeat myself."

I deflated.

I'm not saying you should turn a blind eye to real dangers, you've always got to be aware, but never let one negative portrayal blind your whole outlook. Don't let it prevent you from experiencing something that could be truly amazing or booking a trip to that mysterious country.

Ultimately though, I decided to respect my father's wishes. I dropped the idea of setting up a business in Brazil. I didn't want to remain in India, and I had already quit my job and packed up my life in London. I needed a new plan.

My colleagues suggested I look into Canada. They said the International Civil Aviation Organisation (ICAO) headquarters in Montreal could be a good place to transfer to and I could put my aviation management degree to good use. That made a lot of sense, but French was the main language there. Maneck Aunty would have been thrilled to teach me the language, but I just didn't want to learn another one. It had taken me so long to conquer English – in fact, I'm still learning.

I had also recently visited Montreal to check out Concordia University and decide whether I wanted to study further in aviation or learn a new discipline. Canada was beautiful but I wasn't quite happy there. The weather was cold and dark half the year and it reminded me of London.

I was at a crossroads in my life.

I was no longer sure if I really enjoyed my job at KLM or whether I had just enjoyed the perks. I was still so drawn to IT and the way WebT@ntra had survived over the years. IT felt so familiar, it was really the first thing I was ever good at. I had so many ideas and different possible futures ahead, it made me dizzy. Was I having a pre-mid-life crisis?

Then my friend Shakti invited me to visit him in Australia. The two of us had planned to go to the UK together, remember? But when our visas got rejected, he changed his mind and decided to pursue the land down under. He now lived in Melbourne.

I asked him what any ignorant foreigner does when they encounter someone living in Australia:

"Do you have a pet kangaroo?"

"Have you met the people from Home & Away yet?"

"But there are spiders and snakes everywhere! You know, Australia has the most hostile animals in the world!"

Shakti laughed.

"Honestly, Nilesh, I'm telling you, they call it 'the lucky country' and it really is," he said as we spoke on the phone one day.

"It's an amazing place with so many opportunities, people like you will flourish - the job market is good, the start-up scene is picking up momentum, everyone speaks English, and the people are friendly," he said. "And the weather? Much better than India and London combined!"

I tested the waters with Father. I told him how Shakti had been successful there and that he had invited me to visit. Luckily, there hadn't been any documentaries about Australia, and he had only ever heard good things about it - apart from the snakes and spiders. But snakes are one of the five sacred animals in Hinduism, so I got a green light. With his blessings I started planning my next adventure.

I accepted Shakti's invitation and went to Australia to visit him. I landed in Sydney, spent a week there and then travelled to Melbourne. This is where Shakti had studied, married his wife, and now worked. He introduced me to his friends, and we explored the city together. I fell in love with Australia almost immediately and I knew that this is where I wanted to start my next adventure.

Although some years had passed since I'd made the move to London, it hadn't become any easier for Indians to travel abroad, let alone move permanently. I knew the best way would be to head back to university. I started applying for Masters' courses at universities in Melbourne with help from Shakti. But then one night, I ventured down the internet rabbit hole and stumbled upon articles about this place called Perth. It was in Western Australia, and it was the most isolated capital city in the world. According to some, it was also the world's best hidden secret.

I learned that Perth was beautiful and prosperous and that there was only a two and a half hour time difference between the city and Mumbai. That would make it so much easier to stay in touch with family and friends in India, something that I'd struggled with while in London.

I also discovered that Perth was on the coast and tantalisingly close to magical, picture-perfect beaches. Articles I found said the weather was sunny close to all the year round and the city and state were thriving, thanks to a mining boom. I was sold.

It had been nearly a decade since I left Mumbai for London. I was an international student once again, tracing old but new footsteps. I enrolled at Curtin University and secured a spot in the on-campus student accommodation.

I didn't want to experience the same loneliness I had felt during my first months in London, so I quickly submerged myself in

Australian university life. I wanted to make new friends, create new experiences, and discover my calling.

My Key Takeaways

- Always have a Plan B.
- Do what makes you happy but be ready to accept and consider practical advice.
- When travelling, do some research and be prepared. But do not let fear hinder you in making new friends or having amazing experiences. Sure, there's bad people out there in the world, but there's good ones, too.
- It's never too late to start again. If you are no longer happy with your circumstances, change them.
- You should not turn a blind eye to real dangers, you've always got to be aware, but never let one negative portrayal blind your whole outlook. Don't let it prevent you from experiencing something that could be truly amazing or booking a trip to that mysterious country.

Chapter 12

The Lucky Country

"Don't worry about the world ending today.
It's already tomorrow in Australia."
– Charles M Schulz

I had only applied for a short-term course over one-and-a-half years, as it was easier to secure a visa and I needed less money in an account to show the Australian immigration officials. But I soon realised I would need a two-year working visa to earn money or stay on longer than the study period. With the one-and-a-half year course there was no post study work visa, and I would have to go back to India after completing the course, without a Master's degree. I needed to get into a two-year course with a two-year post study visa. This would mean I would have four years up my sleeve - plenty of time to achieve a permanent residency if things in Perth worked out for me.

On the first day of Orientation Week, I spoke to the international student administrator.

"The first day you come to university, and you want to change your course?" she grunted disapprovingly.

"Well, it's better to change my mind now than getting halfway through," I pointed out.

"You will have to go to a course coordinator, the decision is not in my hands." She waved me away, disappearing back into the ocean of students clambering around student services, housing services and student club stalls.

I wanted to switch to a Master's in Management Information Systems, but I had no university education in either IT or management. In fact, I really had no formal IT qualifications whatsoever, just that basic computer course from which I had dropped out of in Mumbai.

"You are saying you have no previous IT qualifications?"

The course coordinator stared at me blankly.

"Correct," I said.

"Right... So, Nilesh - am I pronouncing that right?" she paused.

"Yes," I replied, pointing to my knee for the fourth time that day. "Knee. Knee-lesh."

"Right, Nilesh, why exactly do you want to do a Masters course in something you have absolutely no knowledge in?" She raised her eyebrows.

"Oh, but I have! I have just arrived in Australia, but I have been working in IT since 1999, completing a whole range of projects all over the world," I said excitedly.

"Okay, so where's your evidence?" she said dismissively. I sensed she thought I was trying to deceive her.

"Give me an hour," I said, jumping to my feet. I ran back to my on-campus accommodation, pulled out a folder and returned.

This folder had more than 50 pieces of paper I had collected over the years - including the reference letter from Cipla Pharmaceuticals, that I had fought so hard to get (and now more than ever I was so grateful for my persistence). I had details of website work I completed on the side.

I returned to the course coordinator's office, a sweaty mess. I knew it would be warm in Perth, but I hadn't expected the heat to be this harsh! The climate was unlike anything I had experienced before, so dry and hot.

I pulled out my documents and showed them to the coordinator.

"Okay, okay! Stop! I don't need to see anymore. I have never had any student come to me with so much work experience before - you're in," she said.

Remember, every bit of work experience you have, no matter how small you might consider it to be, adds a stroke to a bigger picture down the track. Save your certificates, letters and references and always keep them on hand.

After speaking to the coordinator, I nearly bumped into two young men standing by the Student Guild stall. We started chatting. It was orientation week, and the area was buzzing. The two of them told me they had an idea and needed a third person. Sometimes you cross paths with the right people and honestly question if you're in a movie - in this case, I was literally crossing a footpath at the time.

They wanted to create an online platform for selling old course books, directly from one student to another. They needed a website but didn't have any funds to get started. I decided to meet with them to talk things over more thoroughly. I ended up holding my first business meeting in Australia at a Domino's Pizza close to campus.

They told me what they wanted and agreed to pay me 500 Australian dollars each for my services and the domain fee.

A few days later we took a potential investor - a PhD student - to our Domino's 'boardroom' and bought him pizza. He loved the idea we pitched and ended up investing 1000 dollars. And that was that. We started the project within the week.

Shortly after classes started, I settled into a routine.

My change of course meant I got better working rights. I was allowed 20 hours a week, and I could get an Australian Business Number to set up a business. I set up an Australian version of WebT@ntra and printed business cards with the number of my new Australian mobile phone, that Shakti had organised for me.

My business cards actually arrived in Australia before I did. I had sent them by post to my student accommodation because I thought it would be a bad idea to bring them in my suitcase. I had seen a TV show called Border Security: Australia's Front Line and I was afraid I'd be asked to turn around and leave if they found business cards in my luggage. What would a student need business cards for, right?

I knew it would be tricky to find employment right away, and I hadn't brought much savings with me, so I was determined to find projects to work on and look for a job. Maneck Aunty kept telling me to save money for 'rainy days' when I lived in London and I never understood what it meant, but it was now very clear to me why it was important to save.

One website project wouldn't even cover rent and groceries for the next month, so in that first week I took a job at one of the campus cafeterias. I remembered the day in London, when I got up early in the morning to go to my job in the airport café and didn't get myself through the door. I wondered what that young man would have said about me taking a job stocking up fridges with sodas and iced coffees. It was hard work and a real backbreaker. I could handle that, but when I was asked to shell eggs for sandwiches, I felt my values would be broken. I stood firm and refused to do it. They fired me.

Shortly afterwards, another student recommended that I take a job filing paperwork with a company that was hiring. It was a long way from campus, and I didn't have a car, but I pursued it anyway. I made a promise to myself that I would not stay there long. I continued to network and look for better opportunities.

My party-days had followed me from London to Perth and I was already familiar with the best spots for dancing in Perth.

Colin was one of the Aussies I had met at a club in Mount Lawley. He later became a great friend. He lent me his car, for which I was extremely grateful. The only catch was that Colin was a plumber, a typical Aussie 'tradie.' It meant I was driving around Perth in a ute (also known as a pickup truck) with pipes stacked on the roof and a mountain of tools in the back. It must have looked funny, as I was usually dressed in a suit and a hat.

Having a vehicle made going to work a whole lot easier. Rolling up to work three times a week in Colin's ute got me a lot of attention. I was quite the sight and Colin thought it was hilarious. He gave me an Aussie nickname, 'Macca.'

I learnt in London that a social life was key to keeping the feelings of homesickness at bay and growing a network fast was crucial. After hearing more about my website and IT background,

Colin gave me a few projects to work on. I joined the international student union at the university and tried to meet people through activities and events.

A friend I met on a trip to Egypt put me in touch with his friend Mark, who was a Perth local. Mark was a true party animal and would often pick me up on the way to events, clubs and home parties. In return, I was what Aussies call his 'wingman.'

One night we encountered an older lady who danced like she owned the club. Her moves were inspiring and Mark, Colin and I took turns having her swing us around.

We chatted away and I started to call her dancing granny. I could only hope to be as active and happy at her age.

Going out, I would always wear the same thing so business people I met, could easily recognise or remember me. I wore a grey jacket over a striped, blue shirt, paired with blue jeans.

When building your brand, you need a 'uniform.' This was mine.

"Didn't you wear that last week?" Mark eventually asked a few months later. "This? No, never," I grinned. It was good to keep him on his toes.

I had only been in Australia a short while, but it was already living up to its name The 'Lucky Country'. I had met such helpful and kind people. Perth drivers can be a bit testy on the road though. While I had my British driver's licence, I practically lived on top of London's train system, and I never had to drive. Perth marked my first time behind the wheel in a western country and people were not always patient.

I had a fair share of beeps, horns and 'get-off-the-roads,' but I was eventually comfortable driving.

I kept the filing job for two months before I got a job on campus in the career assistance centre as an events assistant. This came about when I created a stir at the international student's office one day after discovering that most jobs on campus were performed by local students.

I told anyone who would listen about the difficulties that international students had in securing work, and that I would really need some support from administrators. After making my case for what seemed like ages, they eventually offered me the job.

As it usually did for me, persistence had paid off. I no longer had to drive around in the plumber's ute, and I gave Colin his keys back.

Sometimes you can form business connections in the most unusual places.

I think it's important to carry business cards wherever you go, because you just never know who you will bump into and when. These cards are not just made for networking events. Keep some in your pocket and your wallet, too.

I had met Jehovah's Witnesses once before, in Bergen, Norway, during my travelling days. I was visiting a friend and went exploring without realising how expensive the city could be. I spent about twice the price I would've in London on a plain McDonald's burger. Feeling as if I'd been robbed, I wanted to save money, so instead of getting a taxi back to my friend's place, I started walking in the general direction I'd come from. The road went into a tunnel, under a mountain. There wasn't a pedestrian sidewalk, so I started to walk over the mountain instead. The sun was setting, and I had no idea where I was. I could just make out a group of people walking towards me and shouting out something I did not understand.

"Hi, I think I am lost," I said, waving at them.

"Where are you heading, friend?" one of them asked.

"To the city, over this mountain," I said.

"Oh, you can't walk over there!" another one exclaimed. "You'll find yourself missing if you try to walk over it, it is too far and without any paths. Let us take you to the bus stop."

These people were very friendly, too friendly. Did they want anything from me?

Along the way they told me about how God must love me, placing me in their path.

I was confused. Who were these religious people? They showed me photos of Jesus - Him I did know about. I had met him in Mexico.

During my travels, I enjoyed meeting people from different religions, listening to their songs and teachings, comparing them to my own Hindu upbringing. Mosques, temples, synagogues and churches are some of the most incredible and breath-taking buildings in the world.

But I'd never encountered spiritual people quite like this. They invited me to what they said would be a 'fun evening' filled with music, a few days later. They gave me the address before they put me on the first bus to Bergen.

I didn't make it to their fun evening, but our paths crossed again during my early days at Curtin University. I was taking my evening stroll, and following the sound of singing, I arrived at a place called Kingdom Hall.

I walked in as if I belonged - I had grown accustomed to entering all kinds of places of worship as if I was part of the congregation.

Everyone was very welcoming and kind, and generously handing out leaflets. They called themselves Jehovah's Witnesses.

I realised they were from the same religion as the group of people I met in Norway a few years back. It didn't seem to matter which country they were from, friendly must have been in the religion's DNA.

There were at least fifty people in the room all singing and clapping - the majority adults. They were very well dressed and used iPads for the hymns. There were lots of fancy cars parked outside and it seemed like the perfect place to network. I handed out my businesses cards and visited the group for the next three weeks. I later learned that Jehovah's Witnesses generally only do business with other Jehovah's Witnesses, but it was not a wasted opportunity. I managed to get two projects from the happy circle, and I had great food, enjoyed their company and immersed myself in their music.

No matter how different opinions and perceptions of truth may be, singing - or music - seems to be a universal trait in religion. As a child I used to love listening to religious music. Both Hindu and Christian. It took me to a happy place, and I was reminded of that at Kingdom Hall.

One of the first risks I took when I arrived in Perth was sneaking into a women's mining conference. Western Australia is a state rich in mineral resources and home to some of the largest and most profitable mining and natural resource companies in the world, so any contacts and networks you can make in that industry can really put you ahead of the curve.

In 2012, I was invited by a student committee to attend an Australian Computer Society dinner in honour of Dennis Moore - the father figure of supercomputing in Western Australia. At the time I remember thinking how big an opportunity this was - anyone who was anyone on the IT scene in Perth was going to be there. Being the new kid on the block, I had to make a good impression. I had just arrived in town, and my pockets were relatively empty. A friend from university helped me find a cheap, rather ill-fitting suit. It was all I could afford, and I did not feel good about it. I wished I could look as slick as I had done for my KLM interview.

My friend's sister did her best with her sewing machine to help me, but it turned out I had no reason to worry. Perth people are very friendly folk, and they aren't very judgemental about what you wear It was just my luck that night to meet Michelle Sanford, a Microsoft employee based in Perth. What a dream, I thought, to work for a global tech giant like Microsoft!

It's funny looking back on that now, not knowing how my path would cross with Microsoft just a few years later. Michelle was the industry go-to person in town. She knew everyone and naturally I asked to catch up over a cup of coffee.

She was busy, she said.

I asked again the next time I saw her. Still busy.

But as you've probably gathered by now, persistence is second nature to me. I don't give up easily and I believe in second chances. Like always, my persistence paid off. Either that or she eventually decided I was never going to leave her alone otherwise.

A few weeks after, she texted to let me know she was attending a conference celebrating women in mining. It was too late to get tickets, not that I could afford them anyway. I brainstormed all my options - do I roll up like the paparazzi, hanging around for when she arrived and when she was leaving?

Do I sit in the conference hall, hoping to intercept her on her way to the ladies' room?

There was really only one option that wouldn't make me look like a complete idiot and that was to sneak into the conference.

I arrived a little after it had started. The names had already been checked off and people were gathered to network over coffee and tea before heading in. I was behaving like a secret agent, staying close to the walls, just as they do in movies. The James Bond soundtrack played in my head as I peered around the corner. Bingo! The coast was clear! And the registration desk was unsupervised. Like a sign from above, a row of unclaimed lanyards twinkled.

I scanned the names; Franny, Rochelle, Lucinda and Sam. Perfect. A unisex name. Choosing that would be easier than trying to explain how an Indian guy came to be named Rochelle.

"It's Hindi for strength," I pictured myself waffling.

The sound of clapping from the event room interrupted my daydream. I managed to walk in bang on a toilet break and the chatty crowd meant I could blend in easily. Well, kind of - I was a man at a women's conference, after all. I spotted Michelle and rushed over.

"Michelle! Michelle!" I called out from metres away.

She was deep in conversation but upon hearing her name, glanced up and did a double take.

"Nilesh... What a surprise.... How the hell did you get in here?" her voice trailed off as she read the name on my lanyard and her stance quickly changed.

"Right, well, you better pretend you belong here now, Sam."

"That's what I am doing, yes," I grinned, mission accomplished.

Michelle ended up introducing me to many of her contacts that day, and after the conference was over, we all headed to the Hula Bula Bar around the corner for drinks.

"You are crazy for making it into the conference to meet me, Nilesh," Michelle said, shaking her head in amusement. We had a great night. I stuck to my H2O on the rocks and met so many great people, some of whom I'm still in touch with today. If I hadn't taken that risk and found my way into that conference, I would likely have missed out on so many important contacts. Important contacts that soon landed me my first IT job in Perth and later helped secure a contract with an education company - Navitas.

In just a few short months, Australia had brought me a lot of good luck and little did I know that in a few weeks' time that luck would strike again. After putting adventures ahead of romance and avoiding many arranged marriage attempts in India, I would finally meet my life partner.

My Key Takeaways

- Ride the wave: take opportunities, listen to suggestions, and always keep paperwork to back you up.
- Don't discard opportunities just because you feel that you might not 'fit in'.
- Be active in student activities. Join clubs, associations, or organisations, and be active in the classroom.
- When building your brand, it can be helpful to create a uniform for yourself. Get a jacket or a coat and keep a certain style for a while. It can help people to recognise you.

Chapter 13

Selecting The Right Life Partner

"Individually we are one drop; but together we are an ocean."

– Ryunosoke Akutagawa

The process of finding the right business partner is very similar to finding the right romantic partner - just without the roses and candle lit dinners. My wife Lene has become both. A helping hand at the office and a solid rock at home.

I met Lene at her own birthday party. I was a tag-along and the 'friend of a friend of a friend.' I was a few months into my Australian adventure when I befriended Ruben, the man who would eventually lead me to my wife. I used to refer to him as STD - Smart, Tall and Dashing.

I had been speaking English for many years at this point, but I still didn't know everything. It wasn't until later that I learned STD was actually a well-known acronym. Thankfully, Ruben wasn't offended!

One evening, Mr. Smart, Tall and Dashing brought me along to a house party near the university campus. It was the birthday party of another Norwegian. I arrived and jumped on to the dance floor immediately, pulling some crazy moves and dancing like an idiot.

I noticed this auburn-haired woman looking a little forlorn. She was about my height, wearing a silky blue top over a dress and her nails were painted to match her outfit. I approached her and introduced myself. We sat down by the kitchen table and spoke for ages. This was Lene, the birthday girl.

She was a little homesick, to which I could relate. I shared a few anecdotes from my years in London in an attempt to make her feel better. I returned to the dance floor to cheer her up with my awkward and silly moves. I put on the song 'Mundian Bach Ke' by Panjabi MC, a proper 'Bhangra' dance and got everyone in a big circle. I taught the party a few fun moves.

It was the one time I wished it was a bar where I was dancing and not at a house party - it would have given me an excuse to pull her away, even if it was to just get her H2O on the rocks.

After that night I wanted to know more about Lene. I added her on Facebook and sent her a message two days later, on her actual birthday and asked if she'd like to catch up for a coffee.

She replied with a short 'thanks' and said she was heading out to the beach by herself. Apparently, it was a bucket list item for her, to celebrate on a sunny beach since all previous celebrations had been on a cold and snowy January day in Norway.

A few weeks later I saw her at my local Westfield shopping mall.

"Oh, hey! How are you?" I beamed walking over to her in the food court. I had visited one of the stores there as I had been hired to redo their website.

"Good, thanks. Nice seeing you, have a good day!" she said quickly, hurrying away.

A tad confused with her abrupt greeting, I turned to watch her walk away.

A couple of weeks later I messaged her about some graphic design work she might be able to help me with for some websites I was working on. She wasn't interested, and said she was more focussed on illustrations and had too many assignments at university to take on more work. I said that that was okay, but it would be nice to have coffee sometime.

This time she didn't even reply.

A few months later, I ran into Lene at another house party. The music was blaring and there was a sea of familiar people sitting around the kitchen and outside by the pool.

She waved from a distance then turned away. I took the hint and struck up a conversation with another Norwegian woman. We had been talking for more than an hour when all of a sudden, Lene cut in out of nowhere.

She asked me to go for coffee the very next day. I was heading to Bali to attend a friend's wedding, but we arranged to meet once I got back.

All the coffee shops were closed by 3 pm in Perth by the time we were ready to hang out. So, I improvised, and we ended up driving to Kings Park, one of the largest and most beautiful inner-city parks in the world. The weather was perfect, we found a bench overlooking the city and watched the sun set and the city light up with glittering and twinkling lights. The conversation between us flowed easily, we had more in common than I thought. But most importantly, she was kind, she was interesting and had an infectious laugh.

"So, I'm a vegetarian," she said.

"Oh, me too! I don't drink," I replied enthusiastically.

"Neither do I! And I don't smoke," she said.

"Wow, I think you could be my princess," I said sheepishly.

It was one of those moments where everything seems to just fit like a jigsaw puzzle and you wonder if the planets really do align and whether chance encounters, fate, destiny - whatever you believe in - have all connected to place this special person on your life path. I experienced all the standard romantic cliches - sweaty palms, butterflies in the stomach, you name it I felt it all. I'd never met a woman quite as incredible as her.

Suddenly, hours had passed in what had felt like minutes.

She kissed me.

And that was all that was needed to light the fire that's still burning bright years later.

I used to form business relationships in much the same way that I formed romantic ones - based on my heart and emotions, rather than my head and logical reasoning. Most of the time they turned out well - until one didn't and that changed the way I did business forever. But I'll get to that.

When it comes to meeting people in the business world, an approach like speed dating can be worthwhile - talk to as many people as possible, find common interests and values and then decide if it's worth taking the next step. I really put myself out there when I arrived in Perth and tried to meet and mingle with as many people as possible.

I networked constantly. I was on my feet all day long, going to every conference, event, seminar and exhibition I could find. I made friends wherever I could and collected what seemed like bags of business cards wherever I went.

I am a firm believer in giving back. It was what my father had taught me. I wanted to volunteer and join committees to help people and organisations make a positive impact. I had already received so much from Australia and Perth, and I wanted to return the favour.

After a bit of networking, I landed a spot on the THiNK ICT Students Association; I joined the Western Australian Information Technology and Telecommunications Alliance committee; became a tech advisor at the local Innovation Centre; and sat on the innovation fund assessment panel in the City of Joondalup. I became a member of the Australian Computer Society (ACS) and I met dozens of fantastic people as interested in technology as I was.

As I have said, networking really pays off. When you put yourself out there – with a stack of business cards handy – you never know who you're going to meet and how they're going to change your life.

This social effort is what secured me a contract with Navitas, an education provider which has since grown to operate in more than 31 countries. The money was good, but I had an itch that couldn't be ignored - I needed a side project.

My Key Takeaways

- You increase your chances of meeting a suitable life partner by sticking to your values.
- Regularly connecting with friends and socialising is a good way to develop your professional network, gain business contacts and meet romantic interests.
- If you're passionate about something, become an advocate for it. Join panels, committees and other organisations dedicated to developing and sharing your interest.

Chapter 14

Giving Back

"Life's most persistent and urgent question is, 'What are you doing for others?'"
– Martin Luther King Jr.

One evening Lene and I went to an event at the Chamber of Commerce and Industry, and that's where I met the Western Australian chief scientist at the time, Professor Lyn Beazley.

Lyn is easily one of the most amazing people I have met. She is kind, an avid Tweeter and a great conversationalist. She also used to attend almost every event I went to and kept introducing me to people.

Meeting Lyn that evening gave me one of my lightbulb moments – the PostCare App. It was one of my earliest Perth-based side ventures and it popped into my head after I took a photo with Lyn. I thought it would be cool to send the photo to Maneck Aunty, but as a postcard.

The best part was I already had a domain name - sendemailbypost.com - thanks to a mistake at the university. I was working on an assignment which involved process mapping, and I accidentally wrote 'send email by post' instead of 'send letter by post.'

So, with a few details already ironed out I started planning what would become my very first social enterprise.

I learned about Good Sammy's when I was looking for a car. It was advertised on one of the notice boards at the local grocery store next to my campus. It was a second-hand store selling affordable clothes and homewares. For a student on a budget, it was a treasure.

Good Sammy's also had social inclusion and employment programs in place to engage people living with disabilities in meaningful work. I thought that would be a fantastic fit for my app. I would donate the proceeds to Good Sammy's every time a postcard was shared and also support employment for Western Australia's disabled community.

Lene came up with the name PostCare App, the logo and a slogan to match: Community care with every share.

It was perfect - and went down a lot better than the first time we had worked together. I almost had a heart attack when I asked her to redesign my logo and my business cards.

I always had WebT@ntra as a business on the side, with an offshore office in India led by the most helpful IT manager I had found, Rakesh. Now that I was in Australia, I wanted the business to get a makeover so I could really drive it forward.

I changed the name from WebT@ntra to Tantra Technology, to reflect the fact that we did more than just design websites and I wanted to freshen up other aspects of the business, too. Because Lene was an illustration and design student at Curtin University, I asked her to spruce up my logo and business cards.

She spent a good few weeks working on it, and a true artist, she liked to play her cards close to her chest. I kept asking to see what she was doing but was told to wait and trust the process. Finally she told me she had three concepts for me to look at.

We sat at my kitchen table, and she opened a folder. I nearly fell off my chair.

She had cut my logo in half!

I was very proud of the logo and didn't like the drastic design change at all, but Lene made her case, and I could see why the image would be a good fit.

Sometimes we feel strongly about something because we have invested a lot of time and energy into it. We are reluctant to see change or let somebody else take the reins. But a fresh pair of eyes can see a lot of things that you have overlooked. For me, Lene was that fresh pair of eyes.

Even in the early days of our relationship, she and I were a good match – personally and professionally.

Once the basic plan for the PostCare App was in play, the next step was engaging the charity I had designed the app for. I picked up the phone to get the ball moving.

"Hello, welcome to Good Sammy's, can I help you?" a lady's chirpy voice sung over the line.

"Hi, I would like to speak to the CEO please," I said, getting straight to the point, in my thick Indian accent.

"He's in a meeting," she said, giving the typical reply a receptionist gives to ward off strangers like me. "Can I take a message?"

"Oh, it's very important," I had to think fast on my feet. I knew I'd never get through otherwise. I also knew that I could be mistaken for someone from a call-centre due to my thick accent.

"Sorry, who am I speaking with?" she said. I could sense from her tone she was starting to get a bit annoyed.

"It's highly confidential and it's very important, please ask your CEO to call me back on this number. Thanks!" I said, hanging up for dramatic effect.

I have since used this method to get past gatekeeper receptionists - feel free to give it a try.

By some luck, the CEO called me back after a little while and I presented him with my idea. We arranged a face-to-face meeting.

I went down to their head office wearing my businessman's hat the following week and told him about the PostCare App. We discussed commercial aspects – 5 dollars for the international fee and 3 for local postage - and support for their employment program. I said the PostCare App should also create a sustainable stream of income for them.

"This is great Nilesh, but what percentage will you take from the earnings? And what will you charge us for using the app?" he asked.

"No percentage, no fee - I will deliver the software, I will make the app, then the enterprise will be yours to run and manage, with every cent of profit yours for the keeping," I said smiling.

"Are you saying you're just going to give us everything?" he said, eyebrows raised.

"Exactly," I said leaning back in my chair, arms folded.

"But why?" he was dumbfounded.

"Why not? Is it not normal to want to do something for the community without asking for anything back?"

With all my off-campus activities, I didn't have much time to spend at university. I never missed a lecture or a group assignment workshop, but I was wasting too much time whizzing from one end of the town to another in my shabby Toyota Camry. Since most of my meeting and networking events were in Perth's City Business District (CBD), I decided to switch universities.

I found Edith Cowan University's Mount Lawley campus was just a few minutes' drive from Perth CBD. So, I enrolled at ECU just before my second semester started. And luckily, even though I had no formal qualifications in IT, they let me keep the same course.

Now I was living in the city, studying in the city and setting up my business in the city. I upped my game and attended more and more events, especially in the start-up hubs and communities. They were popping up everywhere at the time and were full of so many interesting people with ideas and ambitions. I met as many of these people as I could, handed out business cards and felt re-energised after meeting every single one of them.

When I next saw Lyn at another event, I told her about the progress of the app project. She was excited to hear about the social cause and the fact that you could send postcards using your phone.

Truly thrilled with her reaction I heard myself say: "Do you want to be the ambassador for the project?"

She accepted on the spot and began to actively promote the PostCare App around Perth. With this extra push, I gathered a team of volunteers, from the university and the network I had built through committees and associations, to help test, design and develop the app.

I was also able to convince Fuji Xerox to donate a printer for the cause. It was decided that the production would operate from the Good Samaritan headquarters in Canning Vale.

By the time the app was ready to launch, whispers of the PostCare App spread like wildfire - never underestimate the power of word of mouth!

A few months later, on the International Day of People with Disability, we launched the app. We held a small function of about 100 people at one of the Good Sammy's UnitingCare church spaces. Attendees included not only a whole host of non-profit organisations, but also ICT leaders, CEOs, mayors and a high-ranking Microsoft employee (think about it; Microsoft launching an app designed for Apple devices!)

Our hard work got us an article published in the local newspaper, and sparked interest from the Western Australian Governor. He gave all the PostCare App volunteers a certificate of appreciation for social enterprise. Off the back of all the PostCare hype, Lene and I started getting website design work - demonstrating that sometimes, when you give back expecting nothing, good things will return to you in due course.

The PostCare App network laid the foundations for my IT and website design business, Tantra Technology, to do well in Perth. We received more and more work and moved into mobile app development.

At that point, it was just the two of us running the business and we had no office. Lene and I had moved in together at this point, and we had a small studio apartment in the city. Rent was quite expensive, and we got all our furniture second-hand. Her laptop died shortly after she graduated so we invested in an iMac for her to do graphic design. She usually worked from the apartment, and we would attend events and parties to build our client base.

One of these events was a panel of start-ups, hosted at one of Perth's many co-working spaces. One person was complaining about the lack of developers and skills in his immediate network/ onshore and how it was holding up his game design.

"Why don't you use offshore developers in India?" someone shouted from the crowd.

"Well, India... it's cheap and nasty, the developers over there are crap," he said.

I was at the back of the room, standing among a hundred or so people. I thought that it wasn't right to generalise a whole country from one bad experience he may have had, and I felt put off. But even more I felt I needed to speak up. So, I did.

He gave a small nod in my direction, I took the cue and began to speak without hesitation.

"Hi there, my name is Nilesh, I'm from India. You know, you get what you pay for. Paying cheaply means, you get cheap products."

I felt the attention in the whole room shift.

"There are plenty of qualified developers in India, too. Did you know that many successful international companies use Indian-based developers, including NASA and the multinational bank Barclays, just to name a few?"

I paused.

The room fell silent.

"Yes, it's true," I continued.

"They outsource a lot of their work to India. Why? Because it's the world's IT hub in terms of schools and so if those large companies and others can get so much done with these so-called, sub-par Indian developers, why are you having difficulty? Maybe it's not a reflection on their skill, but the price you are willing to pay for quality. It's the same here in Australia. Did you ever consider that?" I waited again for a response, paused for a few seconds, and continued.

"You can't just call a whole country cheap and nasty; you can't apply a blanket term to one bad experience you had."

"My apologies... I...." he trailed off and shrunk away embarrassed, his face turning the colour of freshly picked vine tomatoes. The mediator stepped in and changed the topic.

"Well, good for you for standing up for India," the guy standing next to me leaned over and whispered under his breath.

"I like what you said, Nilesh, I like that you shut him up. From what you said I understand that you have a company. Where's your office? I'd love to come by one day."

"No, well, actually, no I don't," I said. "Not a formal office anyway – I work out of cafes and hotels," I elaborated. "I go wherever people want to meet, so every day is different. As long as I have Wi-Fi I'm fine!" I grinned at him, patting the laptop I had under my arm.

"Well, come see me at my office," he said and smiled while giving me his business card. Graeme was the founder of a security start-up, specialising in cloud technology that prevented malware. This was during one of Perth's mining booms, when office space was hard to find.

A few days later I did go to meet him, and we soon became good friends. He liked what I did and believed in the future of Tantra Technology and within weeks, I began working out of Graeme's office on Havelock Street in West Perth.

I received several offers to work from multiple co-working spaces, which were popping up on almost every corner due to the lack of office spaces and the booming start-up scene. The start-up scene was really taking off in Perth, but as they were focused on raising funds and securing investment before designing a single solution, I didn't feel that I fit in. I never believed in selling my ideas or having to rely on 'founding partners' to see an idea come to fruition. I would always find a way to solve my own problems.

So, I happily started conducting my meetings from Graeme's office. Having a desk to go to every morning also gave more structure to my days. It was a good starting point for me and a testament to how the start-up community outside supported each other.

Graeme would later become my best man at our Perth wedding and is still a very good friend.

Since business for Tantra Technology was picking up, we planned to create a Tantra Design division so Lene could excel in her craft. After a few months I was approached with an opportunity to enter a partnership, and we took it. I needed a person on the ground with me in Perth, who had more technical knowledge than me, and between the three of us things were going well - until they weren't.

My Key Takeaways

- Dedicating some of your time to volunteering or helping your community is very important. It is good for your mental health; will make you feel positive and will help expand own network.
- Leverage your strengths to make a difference. Charity isn't always about soup kitchens or canned food drives. Identify what you're good at and use that to support people.
- Shop at places that sell pre-owned goods! A lot of fantastic items in decent condition can be found at second-hand stores. Be thrifty.
- Let a fresh pair of eyes look at your work and be open to criticism and recommendations.
- Challenge prejudice. It might be uncomfortable, and it might make people stare, but it's important to advocate for people who are being treated unfairly.

Chapter 15

The Highest Of Highs

"If you can't feed a hundred people, then feed just one."
– Mother Teresa

I was feeling very confident in the business after entering into the partnership, and I was probably a little bit cocky, too. We were making good money, having a great time going to events and parties and I was in love with Lene, my soon to be bride.

I had recently gone to India while Lene remained in Perth for a few weeks, as my brother's son was to have his first haircut and in Hindu tradition that is a significant event. I was needed back home for that, and I also had another task at hand; to tell my father I was in love and that I wanted to marry outside of my community.

Before leaving I had told her that it might not go the way we wanted but if the idea of marrying her was rejected, I would not marry anyone else, and we would stay together but not as a married couple.

Never before had I ever felt as exposed in front of my father as I did at that moment in the car, when we were leaving the venue where my nephew's ceremony had taken place. I thought it was now or never. You see, my father is almost never alone as he is surrounded by friends, family or other community members at all times. Being in the car alone with him was a rare event and I told him I had something to say.

I told him everything - that we had been going out for six months and that I really believed this was it.

I do not know why, but I started to cry, and he placed my head on his knee, just like he had when I was a child. Only now it was because of a life-altering decision and not a grazed leg after falling off my bike. I think I was feeling this raw because I was afraid he would not support me, but also because I realised that going down this path would most likely mean that I would never return to India to live. It was a lot to take in, for both him and me.

I felt like a five-year-old, lying there on my father's knee and having my head stroked by his big hands. Funny how it felt different but exactly the same.

"It is your happiness that is important to me, son. The engagement will happen in July next year," he said.

The next few months went by in a blur.

We went to Norway to spend time with Lene's family and get their blessings for the engagement, and then to India to meet my family straight after. The engagement took place in July as my father had decided in December the year before.

I graduated with high distinction in Masters for Information Systems from the School of Business and Law at Edith Cowan University in August 2014. It was only fitting that Maneck Aunty came to the graduation ceremony. I was incredibly proud that day, not just because I had graduated with a Master's degree from an international university but also because I was selected to be the Mace bearer. To be bestowed this honour was beyond belief, more so because I was given a seat on the stage. I made a point of wearing funny socks and the absolute best part was when I was holding my Master's degree, with the two most influential women in my life standing on each side of me.

Maneck Aunty spent three weeks with us before going back to India.

We returned to India two months later in mid-October, to celebrate Diwali with my family. Lene and I took a pre-honeymoon holiday as we figured we would be too exhausted after the wedding. We travelled by car, train and bus to Delhi and Agra to see the Taj Mahal, Jaipur and Amritsar. These are some of the most visited cities in India and with good reason, too!

The wedding was due to take place in Rajkot in mid-December. It was going to be a big wedding, as I was the last in my family to get married. With the extension of my sisters' and brother's in-laws as well, we were expecting quite the crowd. Mumbai is too densely populated for bigger wedding grounds and very expensive, too. Rajkot was the best option, and even more so because of the family ties.

The wedding date was picked after consulting the stars and our horoscopes, true to Hindu tradition. The days leading up to the wedding had a fun-filled schedule. There were traditional ceremonies, dancing lessons, shopping for traditional clothes and time spent with family and friends.

One week before the wedding, Lene went to stay with her parents. It is not common for the bride and groom to live together before the wedding and we wanted to adhere to tradition as closely as possible, so we didn't see, speak or even text each other during that time. We booked a beautiful resort for her family and the many guests we had coming from all over the world to attend the wedding. To fit everybody in, we almost had to rent out every room they had!

One morning I snuck out of the house and took my brother-in-law with me. I wasn't supposed to leave the house at all, as a precaution not to meet with any accident or get injured just days before the big event.

My brother-in-law and I took the car and headed out into the crisp winter morning. The street was not too busy yet and it was all very serene. I was looking out of the window and observing the activities of people setting up their stalls for the day along the roads. We drove past the same spot where I learned how to make toasties 20 years ago and I recognised it as the same stall! We also drove past a group of cows having their breakfast. They were contentedly chewing on grass and hay laid out for them. Taking care of the cows in my hometown Rajkot, was really a community effort and people took turns feeding them. They looked very peaceful and happy and just doing their own thing, as usual.

Soon the traffic would be buzzing around them, swerving and weaving the way traffic in India does, but the cows would still have the same gentle expression, chewing their grass and minding their own business, not paying attention to the chaos surrounding them. I was thinking that Lene and I had been very busy the last year and things had moved so fast for us.

Looking at the cows made me remember Gandhiji's quote I'd seen in the London Underground a few years back; "There's more to life than increasing its speed."

Maybe Gandhi had realised exactly this while walking around the very same streets so many years before?

"So do you want to go to this one here or the next one?" my brother-in-law asked, and I snapped out of my daydreaming.

"Sorry, what?"

"You dragged me out of bed this morning to help you get cards and flowers, remember? You made it seem like it was a matter of life and death, so now tell me; this one or the next one on the next street? I could have slept one more hour, you know!"

I didn't want to annoy him so I picked the closest one.

I went straight to the card aisle and searched for the perfect messages. After a lot of "Is this good enough? Only the best for my Lene!" "Will this say 'I love you' better than this one?" and "No, this is too small", I got the five biggest cards I could find, one for every day until the wedding. We went next door to the florist, and I handed over the cards along with instructions to have them delivered with a bouquet of fresh flowers to my bride's door - one bouquet with one card for each of the next five days.

On the morning of the wedding I woke up early. I hadn't slept very well and had been lying awake for some time. I was excited for sure, yes, but also because I was covered in a now quite crusty turmeric, sandalwood and curd paste. The last ceremony performed before any Hindu wedding is the 'haldi ceremony,' literally meaning 'turmeric ceremony'. It was about giving you good luck and cleansing your past, making sure that you are free, clean and fresh for the next chapter in your life.

The wedding ceremony wasn't until 6 pm, but the day was full of events. There was one more ceremony to be performed before a big group lunch with guests and family members, who had stayed with us overnight. After eating like a king, I was chaperoned off to the parlour to have my hair done and to get dressed. I would arrive at the wedding venue on horseback, and to be honest, I am not too fussed about horses. But a tradition is a tradition.

Luckily, this wasn't the first wedding for the horse, just for me, and it showed exemplary behaviour.

I had a great view of the big parade following me, in front of me, surrounding me. It was a blaze of colour, movement, and sound. There was a marching band in front and all the guests looked magnificent in brightly coloured Indian garments and sarees. They were swirling around me in traditional dance moves. (Lene later told me that she was the only one not to have received any training before the dance events!)

After almost two hours of partying our way towards the wedding venue, we arrived. There were firecrackers, drums and a sea of people cheering and dancing, but I saw only my bride standing there waiting for me.

She was dressed in a white saree and holding a garland of flowers in her hands. Suddenly, both of us were whisked off the ground, lifted and brought towards each other. In Hindu weddings, the bride must 'catch' the groom by placing the flower garland over the groom's head. After four or five attempts she made it, and I was officially caught.

The wedding ceremony itself was extraordinary. I had attended many weddings as a child before, where I gate-crashed along with my sister just to have some of the amazing food. We would dress up and go to all kinds of events, acting as if we belonged. This was actually more common than you'd think! Once, we gate-crashed a wedding and stuffed our mouths full of delicious cakes and sweets. Another guest came over and asked; "So, are you with the groom or the bride?"

"The groom!" my sister said, at the same time as I exclaimed: "The bride!" Laughing and shaking his head, he realised what we were up to but left us to it.

What made this wedding so special, apart from being mine of course, was the diversity of people. We had people from all walks of life, and I was ecstatic they had all gathered to celebrate my marriage to Lene.

The last day of the wedding was the biggest one, with around 3,000 guests. The day after, some of our international guests started to depart and within a week we were back to normal. Lene and I went to Mumbai to spend a week at a resort and rest before heading back home to Perth.

We were riding the honeymoon high when we arrived in sunny Australia again, but it wasn't long before we were brought crashing back down to the ground and to reality in one fell swoop.

My Key Takeaways

- Don't be afraid to ask or advocate for what you want, even if you think the person you're speaking to won't be receptive. People can surprise you.
- Stop and smell the roses. When you lead an active lifestyle, it's important to take moments to relax and spend valuable and irreplaceable time with loved ones.
- It is good to be open minded, but not so much that your brain falls out. Be careful whom you trust, especially in money matters or business.

Chapter 16

From Borderline Homeless To Borderless Gandhi

"Strength does not come from winning. When you go through hardships and decide not to surrender, that is strength."
– Mahatma Gandhi

We had been doing so well that last year or so, with a booming business and an ever-growing network of friends. We returned to Perth after three months in India, excited to continue the Tantra Technology journey and our life together. We had left the business in the hands of our partners while we were away, as they had agreed to carry most of the load while we visited India to get married.

We arranged to meet up the day after we returned to Australia to catch up and plan for the months ahead. But our happiness was soon dissipated. In the following days we made several unpleasant discoveries, and to cut a long story short, like many business ventures, it didn't work out. We found ourselves without a business, without work and without any income. The business accounts had been emptied, our team hadn't been paid their salaries for months and projects had not been attended to.

I had drained our personal savings accounts to pay for a lavish wedding, and we were left with a mountain of debt. Suddenly, we had no income at all and bankruptcy to deal with.

This new life I had created in Perth was slowly falling apart, all because I had committed to the completely wrong business partner.

After losing the business I spent months trying to make it right with our clients and my old team. I managed to repair some of the relationships, but some were lost forever. It was all very depressing, and it was the toughest time for us and for our marriage. We hit the rocks and we hit them hard, but with lots of patience and by taking one day at a time, we overcame it all.

I realised years later, it's the things you co-create that bring you closer together more so than anything else.

Borderless Gandhi became a voluntary and personal project that kept us busy and motivated, a reason to get up in the morning as we were both without work. I kept meeting and helping people where I could, and I was still on various boards, committees and judging panels, but our main gig was our social organisation.

Just before returning to Perth, we attended the Vibrant Gujarat Summit, an initiative by the Prime Minister of India. It was a platform for brainstorming global socio-economic development ideas, sharing knowledge and forging partnerships.

Tantra Technology had been doing well, and I wanted to explore opportunities for us to expand and to create a network in India while we were there. Attending the Vibrant Gujarat Summit was an amazing experience. We ended up sitting on a couch drinking Coca Cola with Ajay Banga, the CEO of Mastercard. We shook hands and exchanged a few words with Ban Ki-moon, Secretary-General of the United Nations and took a photo with Mukesh Ambani, the Chairman of the Reliance Group and one of the most successful businessmen in India.

It is also where we met the Delhi-based artist Vibhor Sogani, who exhibited his stainless-steel sculpture series 'Mahatma in Me'. Lene and I were very impressed with these sculptures and as both of us are admirers of Gandhi's work and teachings, we decided to create a platform that would spread his message further and promote peace, equality and nonviolence.

We wanted to portray these messages by showcasing the life, work and legacy of Gandhi. And what better way to do that than through art, a universal language of the world!

Instead of freaking out or wallowing in the sorrow and despair of being without jobs and having our plans ripped from us, we immersed ourselves in setting up Borderless Gandhi.

Sometimes you need to fall to bounce back again even stronger. You never know what's around the corner.

The biggest issue we had was that Tantra Technology was supposed to have sponsored my permanent residency in Australia. Not only did I have to find a job, but I had to find an employer willing to sponsor me. And I had to find one fast. I had an enormous amount of pressure on me, as Lene's stay in Australia also depended on me. She had returned to Australia after her graduation on a working holiday visa and after we got married, she became dependent on my post study working visa. Living with this uncertainty of not knowing where we would be this time next year, was awful. We were running out of time, and I had to sort out our permanent residency as soon as possible.

I continued to participate in industry events and in a way, I was busier than ever. I attended events all through the day, from early in the morning to late at night. I sat on many boards and committees and my network continued to grow. I had been helping people expand their own networks, connecting people who were looking for positions to fill and those who needed jobs. Networking is very important if you're an international student, and even more so when you're looking for a job. You can fill out all the job applications you want on job search websites, but you will (most likely) not find work there. At least not a position that will help your career.

Or you can do what I did, you could consider getting an Australian Business Number and start working contract roles that use your skill set. You might have to work well beyond the 9 to 5 grind, but it is worth it in the long run.

Between all this, I still made time for those international students, migrants and locals who continued to contact me through friends of friends.

Even while in deep trouble myself I helped people sort out their problems. Not many people knew of my situation, I'd still take them out, pay for their coffee and help them in whatever way I could. Just as I had never made it obvious that I was a student, I didn't go out there and behave as if I was unemployed or desperate for a job. I realised that I had something in me that attracted people and that I was able to help others, no matter what - even when being in greater need myself! Somehow this gave me confidence, and enabled me to relax a little, believing that we would be fine.

We secured Vibhor Sogani's artworks to be shipped from India to Perth, sponsored by the Consulate General of India in Perth and the Indian Council for Cultural Relations (ICCR) in Delhi. We set up a website for the upcoming exhibition, applied for funding and sponsorships from the Western Australian government, the City of Perth and a handful of universities and private organisations.

We landed a fantastic location with the support of the Metropolitan Redevelopment Authority at the brand new Elizabeth Quay, along the Swan River. It was a perfect place for the exhibition, and we decided to officially open on October 2nd, Gandhi's birth anniversary.

Borderless Gandhi was coming to life and articles were being published in both Australian and Indian newspapers. But we were nervous. None of our local sponsorship or grant applications had yet been approved.

I prayed to Hanuman. How would it look if the artworks arrived, and we didn't have the money to pay for anything? Our first event to the outsider would look disorganised and we'd have to answer to the Western Australian government. We were beyond stressed. I didn't sleep.

And then... like a magic movie moment, we received an email from Dr. Ela Gandhi, Mahatma Gandhi's granddaughter. She had heard about our mission and commended our work. We felt this could be the turning point in overcoming all the difficulties we were facing securing funds, and lo and behold; just a few days afterwards, the first grant got approved. Then the second, and the third and the fourth!

The artworks arrived in time along with the artist himself, and two days before the opening, we began the installation work. At 5 am the next morning, we were abruptly awoken by the phone ringing. It was our staging and setup-guy, Tony.

Overnight Perth had been hit by the worst storm in 50 years. All the walls we had put up the day before had blown away and been destroyed. Now we were truly feeling helpless. Looking at the twisted walls lying around the Bell Tower, we felt small, helpless and a short inch from giving up.

Two hours later the site was secured, Tony's crew removed the twisted walls, and we were sitting around a small table at the next-door cafe brainstorming ideas. The storm was still howling outside, wind tearing at the palm trees and fat raindrops hammering down. It is beyond me how the next few hours evolved, but we managed to come up with a solution and the next day we were ready to open the exhibition, on time. The launch was a success. More than 100 attendees and a local group singing traditional Indian songs, including Gandhi's favourite song, came to the event. The next four weeks were full of collaborative events with the WA Museum and various organisations and faith groups who all supported Gandhi's messages.

People have asked me several times, in what way Gandhi influenced my life the most. I think that after the 2016 exhibition, he taught me the true meaning of persistence.

While working on the Borderless Gandhi exhibition, I landed an interview for a corporate print business. I had worked with them previously to produce promotional brochures and business cards for Tantra Technology. I still needed a job, and the company was looking for someone to do business development. I knew my capabilities and backing myself, I laid my demands on the table. Sometimes, you have to be bold.

"I need one month's advance salary," I said to the owner, I told him how I had kept my business running while I was studying in Mumbai and in London, working full-time hours at KLM and when travelling.

If you have a laptop and Wi-Fi you can manage from anywhere, really. I was running out of money and wasn't sure how I would come up with the funds for next month's rent. Lene was trying to do freelance graphic design to help our situation, but very few projects were coming her way.

"How can you ask for an upfront salary when I haven't even given you the job yet!" he laughed, thinking I was joking.

His face fell when he realised I was deadly serious.

"Nilesh, are you crazy? No one in my line of business and in their right mind would ever offer that, it's too risky."

"Your only risk is that you pay me an advance salary and I don't bring in any business in the first month," I said, trying to negotiate.

It took three more meetings like the first one, but I eventually persuaded him and thankfully, within the first week I brought in what would become one of the businesses' largest accounts. I worked hard to rebuild my funds and continued to network for my own gain as well as for the business I was now representing.

Over the course of the months in this role it became obvious to me again that working for someone else was not what I wanted to be doing. I needed to get my own business going again, sooner rather than later. That opportunity came a few months later when I met the man who would later become known as my 'second wife.'

I was at an Australian Computer Society (ACS) event when I got chatting to Vincent Lam, a migrant from Hong Kong, about his latest venture. He was tall and smartly dressed in a black suit and grey shirt, soft spoken and well-mannered. What struck me first wasn't his appearance, though: his brain outshone all his other qualities.

An introvert at heart, Vincent opened up a little more as the conversation flowed and we bonded over exchanging stories from our time as international students.

This guy, I remember thinking, is incredibly smart and spectacularly tech savvy. Vincent had recently decided to leave his full-time job with a successful multinational company to forge his own path and had done just that.

Vincent already had a few prospective employees in sight, mainly a handful of eager undergraduate software developers. But he admitted business development was not his strong suit - he was the tech guy.

I saw my opportunity and ran with it. A week later Vincent and I were discussing the possibility of entering a partnership over coffee at a café situated on Adelaide Terrace. I remember at the time close family and friends warned me - Nilesh, you've just recently seen your last business partnership fail, haven't you learnt anything! Just find a job and forget about running a business!

And in response I'd ask them, "Do you know the story about the scorpion and the holy man?" It's an age-old story about a holy man who sits by a riverbank and rescues a drowning scorpion, but while trying to save the scorpion, it bites him.

The scorpion falls into the water and again the holy man tries to save it - multiple times - despite knowing it will likely bite him again. People ask the man why do you keep trying to save the scorpion knowing the risk of being stung?

The man tells them that it's in the scorpion's nature to bite, just like it's in my nature to help - so why would I not try?

Just because one business fails it does not mean you can't try again if it's in your nature to be entrepreneurial. You can learn to trust again.

After finishing our coffees, I shook Vincent's hand, and the deal was done: a 50:50 split. It's pretty rare to see a 50:50 partnership in business, someone will always generally want the upper hand or more control, but being equal helps to create a true partnership of trust, equal effort and equal gain.

We built a business, that's also a 'family'. But it hasn't all been rosy and smooth sailing - you can't expect to agree on everything. We argue and debate and negotiate. That's the beauty of Yin and Yang - he's the tech guy, I'm the people person. Difference is important for any business, if everyone offered the same set of skills or personality, how could your business connect with the wider world? Like Yin and Yang, Vincent and I are two opposites, we're contrary forces that can be complementary in many ways, but we always manage to agree by the end of the day (or at least by the next day.)

And that's because at our core, we've built something based on a shared purpose that we return to time and time again. It's that same purpose that's resulted in our business gaining international acclaim.

My Key Takeaways

- Persistence pays off.
- If you find yourself unemployed, start side projects to keep yourself busy, this keeps your spirits up and your brain working.
- Picking life partners isn't easy - it's just as important to look for the differences you have, as well as the similarities you share.

Chapter 17

Planting The Seed For A Business

"One man can be a crucial ingredient on a team, but one man cannot make a team."

– Kareem Abdul-Jabbar

Growing a business is very much like growing a tree. But first you must select a seed. And for Vincent and me, that meant being clear on what it was we wanted to achieve.

During our early days, the business had no clear purpose and we had no idea of what it exactly stood for. In 2015 we started out of a tiny office in Northbridge - so small I would often have to take calls from outside. We were a small team, made up of a couple of recent graduates and contractors based in India. Vincent's speciality was Customer Relationship Management (CRM) systems and he had been busy taking on any work he could. I was making phone calls and meeting prospective clients left, right and centre in a bid to build our pipeline of work quickly. At first the business was called CRM Perth, but we knew there was a bigger picture we could paint, and the name might change as we evolved.

Initially, we were open to all kinds of businesses in the CRM space. At the same time, we were growing and adapting the platform beyond simple document or contact management for customer relationships. We leveraged Microsoft stack technology to create one database for client management, scheduling, rostering, call centre management and finance capabilities. I kept coming back to how could we use this for the greater good? I needed some inspiration.

Sometimes the best place to get ideas flowing is somewhere surrounded by like-minded people. I had noticed a challenge in Perth from the day I arrived: its innovation scene operated in silos. This baffled me, as it would surely be beneficial for everyone if they communicated and supported each other? Using my network and gathering a few friends I had made in the tech scene, we created an event that aimed to bring the best of WA's tech minds under one roof, to create grounds for new connections and partnerships.

West Tech Assemblage was launched in 2015, bringing leaders, entrepreneurs, innovators, and government together to promote cross-industry collaboration. The inaugural event was held at Government House Ballroom on Perth's main CBD strip, St Georges Terrace. Speakers included the Chief Scientist of Western Australia, Professor Peter Klinken. In the years since, the event has evolved to focus on themes such as engaging people living with disabilities and the digital inclusion of indigenous peoples. Those events sparked a lot of ideas, but most importantly fostered valuable connections, not just for our budding company, but also other businesses across Perth.

Another great place for ideas is somewhere that has the word 'inspire' in its name.

Each year Microsoft holds an Inspire Conference, where all Microsoft partners gather for a series of events and discussions. It was the first trip Vincent and I took together. The conference was held on the Gold Coast. I was working the room at the after party, introducing myself and making connections.

"Where are you from?" one man in sneakers and jeans asked, above the chatter and background music.

"I'm from Perth, the most beautiful place on Earth!" I replied enthusiastically.

"Are you here by yourself?"

"No, I'm here with my partner... oh look there he is! Vincent! Vincent, come here." The man looked confused, but still happily shook Vincent's hand.

"So ahh... how long have you been together?" he asked, looking back and forth between us. That was an interesting way to ask about our business relationship, I thought. But I figured as English was my second language, perhaps this was just the Australian way.

"Just over a year now, right Nilesh?" Vincent nodded. I saw the man glance at my wedding ring. Then it hit me... this guy thinks Vincent is my life partner! I thought it would be fun to play along.

"Yes, we are locked in," I said pointing to my wedding ring, grinning cheekily at Vincent. He thought it would be fun to play along, too. So, for the rest of the night, we were known as the unlikely, but admired, Chinese/Indian couple from Perth. After that misunderstanding, the story was retold many times and Vincent became known as my 'second wife.'

For my second wife and I, it wasn't so hard to define the purpose or values of our business. I think a lot of start-ups think they must have a value or a mission statement to look good and jump at whatever word is trending, rather than leading with authenticity. For Vincent and me, it was all about our DNA. What did we believe in and live for? What legacy did we want to leave behind and how would we build our eulogy? It may seem absurd to think about what people will say about you after you die, but that can really help you identify what you want, and the business becomes the vehicle to achieve that. It is not what you do that you will be remembered for, it's who you were.

Reflecting on what I had achieved with the PostCare App, and seeing the broader impacts in the community, I wanted to do that again - on a larger scale.

While Vincent was very technical and operational, a superstar when it came to products and development, he hadn't really dipped his toes in forming a big picture vision, strategy, or direction - but I had. I wanted a company that existed to drive social impact, to be much more than just a tech business, something that embraced values of diversity, inclusion and creativity.

Thankfully, Vincent agreed with the idea of a values-driven concept, a tech for social impact element. And it wasn't a hard sell either - coming from a Christian background, Vincent also had an underlying drive to want to do something meaningful. Now we had our purpose, we needed a name. We chose illuminance Solutions.

It largely meant the business no longer looked as if it was limited to CRM. And the 'illuminance' part? Illuminance, by the Oxford dictionary's definition, is to "make (something) visible or bright by shining light on it" or to "help clarify or explain." Basically, our business sought to empower through technology, so other people and businesses could light up the lives of those they served. We recruited Lene as a graphic designer and her creative skills have shaped our brand identity. Her first project was to create illuminance's website. Now we were open for business!

Like most new businesses starting out, we didn't exactly have much to spend on anything flashy - but we knew a website would help us look more professional, and hopefully win us more business. We called in a favour from a photographer friend to take some photos of the team, which at that time was still mostly fresh-faced twenty-somethings straight out of university. A team page would give us some personality, a point of difference in the wave of other tech businesses, I reasoned, and Vincent agreed.

I reminded everyone to dress smartly for the photo shoot. This was going to be great, I thought, all of us looking smart and professional!

It didn't exactly turn out as planned.

It turned out I was the only one who owned a suit jacket and a tie - a yellowish orange tie - not exactly subtle! I didn't want the team to look like amateurs in smart casual get up, so we rotated the jacket and tie between all of us. The shoot turned out with us all looking the same – as if we were members of a jazz band, or about to welcome people onto a plane. It was as if I'd taken a trip back in time to my KLM days and emerged with my own, orange-themed airline crew. But we still looked professional and much older than we all were, which at the end of the day had been the main priority - we knew we had the skills and experience our prospective clients needed, we just had to look the part.

Bootstrapping in the early days of a business can be tough, but it forces you to get creative and have a little fun. From that day on, any time someone came to interview for a position, they were slightly shocked to find us all in different clothes.

There were many times I was asked, "so when do I get the illuminance uniform too?"

Even some of our clients were surprised to not find a row of orange ties staring back at them.

Our first 'big break' arrived when Australia restructured its disability services sector, with the roll out of the National Disability Insurance Scheme (NDIS). The cash flow, organisational structure changes, and new compliance requirements meant one thing: they needed technological help. After some time, we landed our first client in the disability services sector and learnt a lot about the ins and outs of the industry. A few months later, we launched AvantCare, built on Microsoft Dynamics 365 technology. The cloud-based platform tracks every function of a service provider's organisation; from service plan and delivery, rostering, and scheduling to invoicing, recording donations and more. It helps to manage the entire client delivery process spanning from initial contact, care planning and delivery in line with the requirements of NDIS reporting.

Want to know the secret ingredient for building a product? It's finding a common cause. Although we built AvantCare with one client in mind, that digital transformation piece was applicable to many other disability service providers. Rather than building something completely bespoke for one organisation, we built the foundation on a common industry need - to digitally store, record and streamline donations, as well as streamline financial and client management.

It's like baking a Nutella chocolate cake from the same recipe, but it's the icing and decorations that are tailored and personalised. We recognised the opportunity for our technological solution to be adopted beyond people living with disability. We also thought of the aged care sector, which was facing a similar industry restructure.

AvantCare has now been deployed at several organisations, not just in Perth, but across Australia. From one 'seed' it has grown in all sorts of directions, many that Vincent and I couldn't have done alone. That's the thing about planting the business seed - you're not the only one that must water it. In fact, it's better if you leave it alone for a while and let some other people, like your team members, nurture that seed.

The biggest mistakes in business are made when founders become too emotional, or too protective over their tree. Is it a risk to let your team members shape your tree? Maybe. But an even bigger risk could be missing out on input that could make your product or business even more valuable. For example, one of our previous project managers was legally blind. He had a rare genetic eye disorder that obstructed his vision, but that didn't make him any less capable - in fact it made him even more capable of delivering our solutions, as he understood the struggles of those living with the same condition.

Those personal insights enabled him to enhance the AvantCare product offerings in a way Vincent and I never could. Our tree had grown another beautiful branch.

That's not how it always was with us - leaving our tree alone. It's easy to become overprotective and want to analyse every leaf. While I'm mostly laid back by nature and tend to look at the bigger picture of things, Vincent is more of a micromanager. It can be hard to take a step back and let go, so that your business tree can flourish.

But Vincent has a growth mindset and has learned to see the bigger picture, too. We are very different from each other, and just like any other relationship, we have had to work and evolve together.

Play to your strengths - and the strengths of others - rather than trying to do everything yourself. Just because you planted the seed, doesn't mean you'll forever be the owner of that seed or the tree it grows into. You won't be the only one enjoying its shade and fruit, it'll need to continue to evolve without you, to shade someone else and others that follow.

Just like a relationship, a business will evolve, too. There will be growing pains, and there will be times to pivot and make room for change. It took us a couple of years to find our stride with illuminance and what we wanted the company to do for us.

We had achieved Microsoft Gold Partner status at this stage. It meant illuminance Solutions was committed to evolving Microsoft technologies and maximising the benefits that clients receive by expertly implementing their solutions. We'd also designed and successfully deployed our AvantCare solution leveraging Microsoft technologies and for this work we had been nominated in the upcoming Microsoft Partner Awards.

Two months later we received an email: illuminance Solutions was a finalist for the 2019 Global Microsoft Partner for Social Impact award.

We couldn't believe it.

In June 2019, Lene and I touched down in Nevada. All the finalists had been invited to attend the annual Microsoft Partner of the Year Awards and the INSPIRE Conference. Held in Las Vegas, the city is known by many names; Sin City, The Entertainment Capital of the World, the City of Second Chances, and for the next five days; the Metropolis of Microsoft. The awards recognised Microsoft Partners demonstrating excellence in innovation via solutions built off Microsoft technologies, and illuminance Solutions' work with companies that helped people living with disability via AvantCare had stood out to the judges. Sure, the award was great, but what I was really excited about was the chance to meet another one of my all-time heroes, Microsoft Global Chief Executive Officer, Satya Nadella.

Satya was from my home country, an idol and role model for many Indians in leading what is unarguably one of the most successful technology companies on the planet.

Like many, I admired the way he rose to the top in the western world and reshaped Microsoft into a company focused on social good.

His ideology of following karmic management philosophies also rubbed off on me. I was told many times it was simply not possible to meet Satya. He would only be there on the 4th day of the conference, for the keynote address.

I was reminded of the hundreds of companies that had flown in for this event, and the thousands of people who would also like to meet Satya. I had managed to talk to some people in his team and they told me that it would be extremely difficult to have a face-to-face meeting with Satya. That's okay I thought – I had a plan B.

Walking up to the stage at the global INSPIRE conference on the first day, I was a bundle of nerves. I was a school dropout about to accept an award in front of hundreds of the world's most innovative and renowned technology companies, but that wasn't the source of the thundering in my chest. I was most nervous at the prospect of meeting my role model. I had imagined, dreamed and fantasised about the award and receiving it on stage from Satya himself.

After the first few days at the conference, I had let go of the dream of winning the award. There were so many hard-working companies that each seemed very deserving of it. I would have been proud to lose to any one of them.

Being called out in front of more than 20,000 attendees at the T Mobile Arena as the very first Microsoft Global Partner for Social Impact in history was surreal. If I hadn't seen the illuminance Solutions logo flash on the big screen, I might not have got up to walk towards the stage at all, I thought I had heard wrong. But no. We had done it!

When the first winner had climbed the steps to the stage, I realised that Satya was not handing out awards. I was a little disappointed, but I remembered someone had told me he would appear for a group photo with the winners after the keynote address on the 4th day was over. That would be my moment, right?

Wrong.

Have you ever tried competing for attention amid a sea of 41 category winners on stage within the space of 30 seconds?

Exactly.

I revelled in the feeling of celebration nonetheless - it was quite a feat for a little start-up out of Perth to take home the inaugural Partner for Social Impact title. The awards program had received more than 2,900 nominations spanning 115 countries and it felt like a massive accomplishment - I couldn't wait to congratulate the team back home. But first, I needed to meet Satya. I was too close to achieve my dream of many years to let it slip away.

Lene and I had hatched plan B weeks prior.

We had decided she would join me on this trip as the two of us had not taken a holiday alone, since we had got married three years ago. We had gone through a lot in the last few years. We had lost a business, built another and set up many prestigious networking events.

One of her dream destinations was New York and I thought we could go there after Las Vegas, and then to London on our way back to Perth.

One week before we left for the US, Lene started to paint a portrait of Satya that we could give him as a gift. This would be our ticket to see him. As she did not manage to finish the painting before we left, she would have to finish it while in Las Vegas. I wanted her to be as comfortable as possible and found a really good hotel for us to stay, the Delano, Las Vegas.

I found out the chief executives of Microsoft would be staying at the Delano too, as it was practically next door to the T Mobile Arena and Mandalay Bay Conference Centre where the conference would take place.

I picked up the phone to call and make a reservation.

"Hi, I need to make a reservation."

"Yes, sir, of course, what dates are we looking for?" a woman chirped. I gave her the dates.

"Would you like a view of the strip, sir?" she asked.

"What, strip, no, I am coming with my wife!" I said.

"Sir, no," she chuckled, "The strip, the Las Vegas Boulevard, do you want a view of the Las Vegas Strip? You can see the whole south side of it from our hotel, the Luxor Hotel is just next door to us and at night the lights are spectacular. I'm sure your wife would be fine with that."

Leading up to the awards, I made some Microsoft contacts. I messaged them to let them know I had a portrait of Satya that I would like to give him, hoping word would spread to the right person. After a lot of perseverance - and when certain employees saw the beautiful painting Lene had created - I was told the exact place Satya would be at an exact time and wouldn't it just be a wonderful coincidence if we happened to be there too. The only catch? It was an area sectioned off for VIPs. All the winners had been treated as VIPs for the last three days, but when Satya arrived, we were downgraded to normal people again.

The awards and Satya's keynote were considered the main event. About 20,000 people packed the arena and a further 10,000 gathered outside to watch it live on big screens. They were waiting for hours in 45°C under the hot sun. The whole place was buzzing with excitement.

At this point, I had no luck entering the VIP area. It was a booth hosted by Microsoft and only certain stakeholders were invited to see the keynote presentation. I managed to walk in but was quickly escorted out when security staff noticed I was wearing the wrong colour lanyard.

I tried to sneak in again, but they asked my name to see if it was on the VIP list and it wasn't. So, I was turned away again.

I hung around the entrance anyway, checking my LinkedIn messages on my phone and striking up conversations with people showing up who had their names on the list. The chief partner's office assistant came out to see me after some time. She smiled at me and listened to my explanation that I had a painting I wanted to give to Satya. She was friendly and explained that Satya would not be coming to the booth after his keynote speech, but I was welcome to join them in the booth to see the stage from there.

Suddenly, just 5 minutes after the keynote ended and the thunderous applause had died down, Satya's Chief of Staff called me. It all happened so fast. He told me to bring the painting and be outside a conference room in 3 minutes. I made it, but the painting was at the hotel with Lene, so it was just me, out of breath and jittery with nerves.

Meeting him, I tried to touch his feet, as we do with all respected elders in my country.

"No need to do that brother," Satya said, catching hold of my hand and shaking it instead. He started talking to me in Hindi and I was blown away by his humility. I told him I had a portrait I wanted to give him but that I was called up to see him too quickly and I didn't have it with me. He organised with his Chief of Staff to squeeze me in the same afternoon. I called Lene and asked her to bring the painting to the convention centre and the both of us soon handed the artwork over to Satya. We caught him literally in between doors as he went from one meeting to another.

"You made me younger," he laughed when he saw the painting, "And, you gave me more hair!"

Satya has a clear vision and leads with empathy and authenticity. I had admired his values and leadership style for years, especially how he adhered to driving good outcomes for communities. He did not just see Microsoft as a vehicle for profit. Microsoft is extremely successful, but as a result of its business model with social impact at its core.

Although we didn't specifically look to work with charities and non-profits, illuminance Solutions has attracted them like a magnet.

Being the first ever Microsoft Partner for Social Impact, and a small company from Australia at that, we got some media attention. In one article published by the Sydney Morning Herald, I challenged Microsoft to lower their fees for the non-profit sector. It piqued the interest of a CEO from a very respected Australian disability service provider who messaged me on LinkedIn and said if I was ever in Sydney, it would be good to catch up.

"Vincent, this could be a big opportunity for us," I said to him one afternoon.

"Yes… it could be," he agreed.

"I think I need to fly over and meet her. And I'll canvas some more prospective clients while I am there," I said, chuffed with my plan.

"Yes, that's a good idea, but wait for another three months. We're going to a conference in Sydney soon anyway, so you can wait until then," Vincent said. "It's not just the cost of the flights but accommodation as well, you know. We don't have the budget for this short trip right now."

This is where the Yin and Yang of our business relationship comes into play. Vincent, he's the numbers guy - good with money, sensible, responsible and I respect him for that, even though I'll disagree and sometimes tease him for being stingy. I on the other hand… I'm a little more liberal, up for treating employees or spending on things I ultimately think will help the business.

"But this could be huge for us!" I said. "This CEO, she said we were impressive and a potential fit for the technology partner they are looking for. She wants to catch up and meet, you've read the LinkedIn message yourself and you know that AvantCare is a perfect fit for them!"

"It is not wise to spend so much money travelling to the other side of the country, just to go to one meeting, a meeting that's not even set in stone. You know, Sydney is a 4-hour flight from here. And with hotel costs and all, it will be too expensive. We can't do that right now!"

It was a big disagreement, an hour-long heated discussion where we eventually left each other angry and annoyed. I returned home to Lene fuming, complaining about my stingy business partner who obviously had no faith in me or my marketing skills.

"I'm disappointed that he doesn't understand the potential of this meeting - it's about the bigger picture!" I repeated to her. "Yes, it may put us back a few steps in cash flow for the month now, but that one meeting could pay for those airfares ten times over if it goes well!"

We were having dinner, and I was stabbing vegetables with a fork, angrily shovelling them into my mouth.

"Well, why don't you just do what your gut tells you to?" she said, as my stomach gurgled right on cue. I chuckled.

"Not like that!" she rolled her eyes. "If you're so sure about this meeting, what's actually stopping you? Vincent can't stop you. Use your own money!" she offered, nonchalantly, as if it was the most obvious solution in the world. My 'first' wife had a good point, so I consulted my imaginary board of advisors.

Remember that imaginary friend you had as a child? Whether you were happy or sad - it didn't matter, your imaginary friend was always there, especially when you needed someone to turn to for advice. You may have long said goodbye to your imaginary friend.

But I haven't. I have several imaginary friends on my illuminance board, but each and every one of them is very much a real person.

Having a collection of role models or people that inspire you can really help when things get tough, when you're faced with a difficult decision, or are considering disobeying your second wife to fly a couple of thousands of kilometres across Australia because of one LinkedIn message...

My imaginary board members pretty much told me to 'go for it', especially former Alibaba CEO Jack Ma. Jack is who I turn to for resilience. He failed primary school tests, was the only interviewee out of 24 people rejected for a job at KFC and received countless 'nos' from Silicon Valley for funding opportunities. He still created Alibaba, one of the world's most successful companies.

I also consulted the head of my imaginary board, Microsoft CEO Satya Nadella, who I had appointed for leadership advice. I decided if he were in my shoes, he would do the same thing. And that's the point of my imaginary board. I put myself in their shoes and them in mine, walking through their values, their thought processes to think, what would they do?

My imaginary board fluctuates daily, sometimes I add more people to the board, sometimes people leave to go on holiday. But there are two members that have been there from the beginning, who I know I can count on to always be by my side: Maneck Aunty and of course, Lene.

I came back to Earth and quit my daydream - Lene was right, and my imaginary board backed me. So, I booked those plane tickets and secured accommodation for the next day.

"I booked a ticket; I will see you tomorrow. Don't worry, I paid for it myself," I texted Vincent, once I was at the airport early the next morning, ready to board the plane. I turned my phone off so I had a few hours to prepare for his reply.

Thankfully, it turned out my gut was right. Upon landing, the CEO was shocked at first about an impromptu meeting but agreed to chat for half an hour.

And half an hour was all we needed.

Thanks to Lene's solution and my borderline disobedience, we landed one of our biggest, most loyal clients in the disability service provider sector. It enabled illuminance to add more headcount, but most importantly, scale to help non-profit groups.

My Key Takeaways

- Appoint an imaginary board: think of a collection of people that inspire you, turn to them for 'advice', embrace their values, put yourself in their shoes when unsure about tough decisions.
- If at first you don't succeed, try, try and try again - even if that means trying out different approaches to meet your goals, just like I did with Satya.
- Go with your gut feeling! It is usually right.
- You know the saying "what happens in Vegas, stays in Vegas?" It's not true. I took our award trophy with me all the way to Australia.

Chapter 18

Storytelling And Power Point

"Share your knowledge. It is a way to achieve immortality."

– Dalai Lama

I knew nothing about the First Nation people of Australia before moving to Perth, although during my travelling days, I had learned about indigenous people in Canada, the US, Africa and South America.

My first real meeting with Australian First Nation people on a personal level was when Lene and I went to Kings Park to take photos for our wedding invitations. We were enjoying ourselves, walking up and down the park holding hands while the photographer went high and low to get the best shot possible.

I noticed a family sitting in the café and when I locked eyes with one of the gentlemen he waved us over. It turned out to be Dr. Noel Nannup and his family. The man who had waved us over was his nephew, Shaun. Dr Nannup is a highly esteemed and respected Aboriginal Noongar Elder in Perth, and he wanted to know what we were doing. We told him and he told us that the land now known as

Kings Park had always been of great importance and significance to the Whadjuk Noongar people for at least 40,000 years and that it is in fact a place of ceremonial importance, a meeting ground and a place for weddings.

Then he blessed our union by performing a personal and intimate welcome to the country. Lene and I were taken by surprise and felt immense humility when we received this great honour which we will always remember and carry with us.

As I learned more about the Aboriginal and First Nation people, I discovered that indigenous organisations also required some technological help. In Australia, particularly in Western Australia, where mining is a leading business industry, agreements are struck with local communities for use or lease of their land. Mining companies place funds into trusts - known as Native Title Trusts - as payment and benefit to the broader Aboriginal community. In the past many indigenous organisations were managed by third parties, each taking dollar for dollar, often leaving members with less funds to invest directly back into their communities.

We created the Aboriginal Trust Management System (ATMS) It was like AvantCare in that it provided one platform for Native Title Trusts to manage funds and compliance on their own for the first time in history.

The more we talked with indigenous Australians, the more we understood about their history, hardships, and goals as a community.

One of the less talked about struggles is the digital divide between people living in very remote communities and the rest of the country. It shocked me. We were in a wealthy, resource-rich developed nation rippling with technology and innovation yet there were still pockets of the population who couldn't use a computer, tablet or phone. I decided I would try and do something about this.

It was now 2019. Fittingly, it was also the United Nations' International Year of Indigenous Language. West Tech Assemblage had been thriving for the last four years and we were due to hold another event. We decided to dedicate our 2019 event to bringing together local Aboriginal elders and other tech and community leaders. We had a mission: to raise awareness of the digital divide and discuss solutions.

Disaster almost struck when two days before the event, our key speaker, the Federal Minister for Indigenous Australians, the Honourable Ken Wyatt, pulled out. But after pleading on the phone with his assistant (more than once), Uncle Wyatt (as the locals would call him) came through on his promise. He flew from Canberra to Perth for one night only and helped us launch the digital literacy program for indigenous communities that we had designed.

We partnered with the University of Notre Dame Australia to create the program. It was designed to teach computer and internet basics, as well as help indigenous Australians navigate online bills, banking and make healthcare claims.

More importantly we opened the program to non-students and all ages. There are many training programs available for the young, but not so many for seniors, and it's important that they don't get left behind. We decided to roll out the inaugural two-day training program at the University of Notre Dame's Broome campus.

I travelled to Broome with two colleagues and we were warned before arriving "not to expect much."

Stepping off the plane, Broome's warm air was like a comforting hug from home, memories of Mumbai's similar climate wrapping around my mind.

My friend Eric, another Perth entrepreneur who runs his own IT company, had a staff member based in Broome to service regional clients, who also joined us to help with the program. We had advertised the program on the local radio station, in newspapers, newsletters, Broome's chamber of commerce and more, and received about 27 expressions of interest. When we landed, the student activities officer from Notre Dame's Broome campus came to greet us and almost wiped the smiles from our faces.

"We are so excited to be able to teach 27 people, it's a great result, right?" I said grinning.

"Look, even if half of them turn up… you will be lucky," she said. "Whoever does turn up, even if some stay beyond the first tea break, after lunch most of them won't come back, because the dropout rate is huge."

"It was a tough pill to swallow, but as you must have realised by now, I'm not one that gives up easily, nor do I ever let anyone's doubts get in my way of achieving a goal. We hadn't travelled this far and put so much time and effort into this training for nothing.

"Basically, what I'm telling you is, don't have high hopes," she shrugged.

The next day 17 people turned up. It wasn't bad - only 10 no-shows. I considered that a win. It was better than less than half!

We started the day off by asking the mob what they wanted to know and learn - after all, this was a program for them and considering my experience at school, forcing subjects on students wasn't something that ever engaged me. We needed to tailor this to their needs, so they could find the value in the training for themselves.

"How can I find the winning lottery numbers on the internet?" one asked, dead serious.

"We can't help you find that," I said, trying to respect his genuine query and not to laugh, "However, we can show you how to find the trends and patterns that could help you."

One elder wanted to do research on their land. Others just wanted to learn simple navigation of Google and how to access essential services on the internet. The best way to learn is to teach, and it wasn't long before they were all teaching each other about their new discoveries. After the tea break, everyone returned. I tried not to feel smug at this achievement. I was surprised when the group continued to return after each session, hungry for more.

Storytelling is important in Aboriginal culture and arguably the most popular lesson I taught was using Microsoft PowerPoint as another tool to tell stories. I didn't want to put pressure on the group by setting a formal assignment, instead we created an impromptu in-class project with the goal of creating a five-slide presentation: 'Storytelling through Power Point.' I set out the guidelines: presentations had to include a mix of graphics, bullet points, text, a consistent layout and it had to tell a story.

Storytelling through Power Point was a big hit, even if at first both the young and old were hesitant and nervous to present. Everyone came up with a funny story - about a bird, their background or the river and no two presentations were the same, with everyone applauding and proudly beaming, finishing the training with tangible proof that they had conquered some of these once-scary computer skills. When the two-day program came to an end, we finished with 21 people in the class - more than we had started with.

"I have been working here for 20 years and I have never seen such great engagement," the Notre Dame student activities officer said, baffled. "What did you do differently?"

"We treated them like we would treat any other group of students that we teach," I told her.

"We focused on their needs, made it interactive and personalised the training. We couldn't exactly pinpoint the winning lottery numbers, but I think that student was happy enough with what we did provide."

"What?" she asked, a little concerned, probably wondering if we'd shown them some sort of illegal hacking process.

"Never mind, nothing to worry about!" I said. "We simply spent the time learning what it was that they wanted to know and let that determine what we would teach."

I think that is a really important point for education of all types: teaching can be forced, but true learning is really only achieved through self-empowerment.

Even if Vincent and I were running a restaurant business instead of a tech business, our purpose would be the same. We'd be a restaurant that was in some way, shape or form, helping the broader community. Let your business simply be the vehicle for your purpose or passion.

There have been many moments in my life where my belief in karma has been tested and tried, wondering when goodwill was ever going to come back to me, or questioning why bad things would happen to me. Now that I'm older I realise karma is not conditional - it's giving without expecting anything in return.

That being said, life has a funny way of repaying the favour when you do the right thing, especially when you least expect it.

The lessons my father tried to instil in me from an early age stuck with me. I co-lead illuminance Solutions with karmic management in mind. In my mind, if you help others to become successful, you will be successful.

This philosophy helped me realise that I had always received help when I was travelling. If I hit a snag anywhere in the world, someone would appear as if by magic ready to help out. Ready to feed me, help me find a place to sleep or lend me a jacket on a cold day. It was good karma at work.

A few inspirational quotes have stuck with me. Sometimes, you hear something so snappy and poignant, it resonates with you for life.

One of my all-time favourite quotes is from John F. Kennedy. He was trying to explain the importance of civic action and public service and I think he did so masterfully.

"Ask not what your country can do for you. Ask what you can do for your country."

I include this quote in all my presentations or talks that universities invite me to, on the last slide. International students or migrants rarely get the opportunities they deserve, and most often they will settle for doing hard labour instead of utilising their real talents and skills.

Vincent believes in the philosophy of servant leadership, where the needs of the employees are put first, and the leader exists to serve the people. I believe in something similar. In empowering others to achieve your own success. I can almost guarantee that this has propelled illuminance Solutions to the success it is today.

We have prime views over the Swan River from an office on Adelaide Terrace in the heart of Perth's CBD. We employ about 36 people from different backgrounds, cultures, and nationalities. Our services stretch from Perth to cities all around Australia – major capitals and smaller towns.

I was given a fair chance when I came to Perth and now, when I'm in the hiring seat I pay special attention to those who have had to work hard, overcome adversity or simply those who are a little different. We employ qualified migrants and give them a chance to flex their skills in a new, sometimes challenging country. They come from all corners of the world. They are of different ages, abilities and have different life stories. These people power our engine room. For us, diversity has been the key to innovation.

But I didn't always think this way. It was a learning curve.

We are often blinded by our own preconceived attitudes and beliefs so much so that we can overlook the best opportunities - or people. Differences should be celebrated and embraced, not feared. I only recently realised that by employing people living with a disability, we connected with our clients on a level in a way no other company has, our staff representing some of the very people they helped. It was a nice by-product of doing the right thing and hiring the right people regardless of their appearance, gender, ethnicity or disability. We have even won tenders as a result of people with disabilities having designed our products, as they kept in mind their own requirements for accessibility as well as our clients' needs for the same.

Sometimes, life has a funny way of rewarding you for following your heart and doing the right thing.

My Key Takeaways

- You don't have to wear every hat in your business: play your strengths.
- When you immerse yourself in a community and contribute meaningfully, that can be one of the most gratifying and memorable experiences.
- The future of business is leading with the heart, empathy, and purpose. Create social impact for the betterment of society.

Chapter 19

Success Is How You Define It

"Success is a science; if you have the conditions, you get the result."

– Oscar Wilde

Success is like happiness - it all depends on how you frame it. For some, success is getting high distinctions at university, for others it might be passing or gaining a degree.

Throughout the years I have learnt success is malleable and looks different from person to person; it could be a shiny trophy, a six-figure salary, saving up enough money to move to the other side of the world, or simply having your parents say they are proud of you.

For me, success comes in all shapes, forms, and sizes. It's important to cherish these fleeting moments of success and store them as light at the end of the tunnel when life gets tough.

I feel successful whenever I am invited to speak to groups of international students. I am always transported back to the time when I gave lectures at Edith Cowan University to more than 125 Masters' students, when I was a teacher for one semester. It's not bad for a guy who failed school multiple times, not to mention a non-Australian who was almost homeless shortly after arriving in the country.

I also feel successful when I provide employment for someone who needs a chance to prove themselves. It's a common belief that migrants have to start at the bottom of the job market when they move to a new country, even if they have more than two decades' experience in a specialised field. There are stories of migrants who have worked tirelessly as an engineer or a university professor, who had to take a job dozens of notches below their skill level.

Vincent and I hated that, and we have used illuminance Solutions to put a stop to it.

Awards can be another barometer of success. They're an indication you are moving in the right direction, and they can validate good work. On the flip side, they also come with increased expectations and a heightened sense of responsibility. I have had some sleepless nights after receiving awards. I feel that with each and every one we receive, there is less room for error and that we have to perform better and focus on quality even more.

I have also learnt that awards tend to come in groups. If you earn one, you're likely to earn more. After illuminance Solutions received the Microsoft Global Partner for Social Impact award more doors opened for us.

We have now repeatedly been awarded for our commitment to workforce diversity and we have been formally recognised for our high-quality products and services. The common thread that runs through every achievement though is people and how it feels when you celebrate each milestone with friends, family and your team.

Success is often less about the tangible object - whether it be a medal, paper or otherwise - and more about how it feels to share the success with others.

After a few years in Perth, Maneck Aunty visited again with my niece Diya.

Their visit coincided with an awards ceremony that aimed to celebrate migrants and their achievements.

I booked Maneck Aunty and Diya a ticket.

"Uncle, I know you're going to win, I just know it," Diya said excitedly.

"We will see," I said laughing nervously. "Let's just enjoy the night and the food."

We entered the hall and sat down. The award ceremony began. A number of winners in different categories were announced to cheering and applause. I could see my family starting to become disappointed the longer we waited. I was not particularly emotionally invested in winning awards, but I did feel some pressure. I knew Maneck Aunty and Diya wanted to celebrate with me.

"I thought I was your good luck charm," Diya said glumly.

"You certainly are my good luck charm, in many ways. I don't need an award to prove that to me or to you, or to have a great night. Isn't it nice just being here together? And look at all these people doing amazing things being rewarded tonight," I said. "We can learn something from them."

She turned her attention to the stage again, listening to the snippets of stories of these amazing people who had created new lives and success from nothing - it was truly inspiring and with that I felt like the luckiest person in the room; here I was surrounded by greatness. How privileged I was to be able to share that with my niece.

"Ladies and gentlemen, for our last award of the evening, we ask you to put your hands together for the Business Migrant of the Year... Nilesh Makwana from illuminance Solutions!"

Diya realised I had won before I did. She jumped up and down and clapped like mad. I did a double take and realised what had happened. The best part about that award wasn't the award itself, it was bringing my niece up on stage with me and seeing her glow. She was so chuffed and proud of her uncle and seeing her like that was the most rewarding experience. One that money can't buy, and no piece of paper or trophy can convey. It was definitely my most memorable awards ceremony.

The second most memorable event was one I got to share with my whole team.

The grand ballroom at Perth's Crown Towers was beautifully lit and everyone was so nicely dressed. It was one of the fanciest award evenings I'd ever been to, and the room was packed full of the city's most influential people. There were politicians, business leaders, company owners, entrepreneurs, creatives, medical researchers - pretty much the brightest minds of the state packed together in one space. The event was the annual Business News 40 under 40 Awards. Each year the media publication Business News hosts awards that honour 40 individuals under the age of 40 for their business, medical or organisational achievements, as well as their contribution to the wider community.

It was an extremely flashy event, so I decided to dress in kind. I didn't have to look far to find my outfit because it was actually my wedding reception suit, and it was the first time since I married Lene that I had pulled it out of the closet. I wore a purple cravat, which unintentionally matched the decor of the building. The lighting was purple and pink, with a dining area to match.

It's not behaviour I would encourage, but I have to admit, ever since I found out I was a finalist, I tried to learn my chances of actually winning the award.

I was feeling anxious. I was 39 and it was my last chance to even be nominated before I aged out of the category. I had an insider contact - one of the Business News journalists I'd previously worked with, but she wouldn't give me anything and played the poker face exceptionally well every time I pressed for a clue.

"Nilesh, all I can say is it would be very worthwhile if you attended," she winked after I had bumped into her one day. "If nothing else, it will be a great networking event."

Little did I know, she knew all along. She was one of the co-announcers and was given the list of winners a week before the event.

The first half of the winners were announced and there was no mention of my name. This time, there was a little more on the line - rather than just one hopeful cheerleader like my niece Diya had been, I had a whole table full of colleagues and friends, my wife Lene and my second wife Vincent.

Again, it came to the end of the winners, 37th, 38th, 39th. That feeling of letting down the illuminance Solutions team was more intense than the feeling of not winning anything at all. I was worried. Lene squeezed my hand, knowing what I was feeling and thinking.

"Now on to the 40th award tonight, who is also the winner of one of our major prizes - the City of Perth Strategic Alliance Award..."

The MC's voice echoed around the room, everyone waiting in anticipation.

"The City of Perth Award recognises the outstanding success of a person within their chosen field and acknowledges an individual whose motivation, leadership and entrepreneurial spirit has turned a business into a significant and ongoing opportunity for Perth to highlight its expertise, commercial opportunities, talent and liveability."

Oh dear, there was no way this was me, I thought. My journalist friend simply didn't want to break the bad news to me, so that's why she spun the positive side of networking and making new connections. It was all making sense.

"Previous City of Perth winners have come from industries as diverse as resources, professional services, medical health and life sciences."

Wow, there's no way I stood a chance – some of these people had made medical breakthroughs, or commandeered huge mining workforces. Whoever this winner was, they must be pretty amazing. I felt a strange mix between relief and disappointment.

"Tonight, we have that winner. And that winner is... Nilesh Makwana!"

My table erupted into hoots and cheers as I sat there dumbfounded. All around me my team and my business and life partners, Vincent and Lene, were beaming at me. This award was theirs, not just mine. Goosebumps of gratefulness and excitement erupted all over my body.

"Lene, pinch me please," I said, staring straight ahead.

"What?"

"Pinch me."

She did.

Ouch!

Yes. This was real.

This was really happening. One of my colleagues and Lene pulled me up so I could start walking to the stage

"Nilesh is an entrepreneur, social impact innovator and advocate for workplace diversity," the MC's voice rose above the cheers. She read off a sheet that summed up my life in as little as 150 words.

"Arriving in Perth in 2012 with no business or social contacts he co-founded illuminance Solutions. The business has fostered soft diplomacy between India and Western Australia, created the innovation event West Tech Assemblage, and developed and delivered a free training program to boost digital literacy among indigenous communities. Nilesh says he aims to live life with purpose every day, leading the organisation to create technological solutions for social impact. He's also co-founder of WA-based not for profit, Borderless Gandhi. Well done, Nilesh and congratulations."

The applause was a lot louder from the stage, as 500 or so happy faces smiled back at me. "You colour-coordinated with the award!" the MC joked as I made my way off the stage. "Got yourself a bit of a workout there too with one award in each hand," she laughed.

I didn't know what to say, I was still in shock, so I said the only thing that was on my mind at that moment.

"Perth is the best place in the world. A true heaven!"

"I don't think anyone here would disagree with you on that," she said. A new roar of cheering erupted.

In my third favourite awards ceremony, I didn't win anything. Nor did illuminance Solutions. I was pumped up, elated, dressed in my absolute best, feeling like a million bucks. I brought one of our consultants along to a business award where illuminance Solutions had been named a finalist. Maree had been coming to us for workshops and team training sessions for years and she was a good friend.

"We've got this in the bag, I just feel it," she said, confidently.

But this time, the last name announced wasn't ours. Maree was furious, she truly felt deep down that illuminance Solutions was the worthiest, and she decided to nick the floral arrangement from the table as a commemorative prize. She tucked it under her arm and briskly walked out.

Honestly, it was very funny. And looking at her walking out in frustration made me chuckle and plastered a big smile on my face. I was grateful for all the Marees I had in my life. People who had backed me, believed in me, supported me through the highs and lows.

I'll never forget Maree's small tantrum. It's hard to pinpoint why, but somehow it meant more to me than winning an award ever could.

My Key Takeaways

- Success can come in many forms: it's not always about awards or money. Making a lasting, positive mark on the broader community can leave a better legacy than any trophy.

Epilogue

I hope you've enjoyed travelling with me through my ups and downs and that you've learned a few things along the way. I will leave you where we started - on the banks of the Swan River. Today the sun is shining (that's the thing about Perth, when is the sun never shining?) and it will set and rise... and set again and rise again. Remember that. Because when the world is in chaos, when disaster strikes, and you lose everything - materialistic or otherwise - there will be a tomorrow.

The quarantine and isolation that has come with the pandemic have been no easy feat, after all we're social animals by nature. Some coped better than others - take my wife Lene for example, she was more than content to be left to herself, to get lost in books or become completely absorbed in creating art.

I was the complete opposite, I struggled with not seeing my friends, Vincent's cute son (and Vincent too), the local coffee shop people, just anyone else beyond the walls of our apartment for days on end. Sometimes the worst things in life can have a silver lining. For me, those periods of isolation made 2020 an enforced year of reflection. I have always been a go! go! go! person – and having to stop and to be in one place for a long time goes against every grain in my body. To be fair, we did have it pretty easy in Perth, given we're the most isolated capital city in the world. Keeping our borders closed meant life could resume to pretty much normal within a few months, but of course with ramifications to last for years.

For a migrant like me, however, it also meant having family spread across the world to worry about, as all our loved ones were in places that didn't do as well as Australia. Just before the outbreak I became an Australian citizen and I had been looking forward to using my new passport to travel again. In trying to approach COVID-19 with a glass half full attitude, something wonderful came out of it - in Perth at least - which is why I take you back to my happy place, to the banks of the Swan River.

Suddenly, more people came outside. Lene and I ride our bikes or go for a walk along the Swan River loop on weekends, often stopping in South Perth for an acai bowl or a coffee. We noticed the change - without shopping malls, gyms, or restaurants to go to, people flocked to the outdoors.

We have all been reminded of what really is important. I think a lot of people became more grateful and appreciative of the simple things in life. Now it's time to take action.

When news of the pandemic spread around the world, Vincent and I were worried as our business had been flourishing. The economy was starting to pick up again in Western Australia after the mining slowdown around 2013 and suddenly, literally out of nowhere everything hit pause overnight.

Like many business owners I am sure, I was troubled and scared. Some of our clients pulled out of early conversations and others came to a screeching halt. How on earth could we bring money through the doors if no one wanted our services? How would we be able to keep our team members if we lost clients? Having to let people go is for me the worst thing about being a CEO, and every time it happens it affects me deeply.

Stock markets worldwide quickly went into shock. Panic can do terrible things to people, it can bring out the worst in humanity, prompt poor decisions, spread misinformation, fuel discrimination and despair.

Trying to put panic aside, Vincent and I took a deep breath, put on our thinking caps, and pivoted fast. We designed an emergency response module for AvantCare. We worked with clients trying to remain connected to their own clients. We worked with Chemo@ Home, a private health organisation that administers chemotherapy for cancer patients from the comfort of people's homes rather than in hospitals.

With coronavirus a threat to the immunocompromised, hospitals became too risky an option. Chemo@Home expanded its services across Australia and engaged illuminance Solutions to support the digital expansion. So, while 2020 didn't end quite as expected, it definitely ended a lot more positively than initially anticipated. For a fact, if the pandemic hadn't happened, I may never have started to write this book - otherwise too caught up in the day-to-day busyness of daily routine.

And what a missed opportunity that would have been.

Leaving your home country to put down roots in another is a terrifying experience. No matter the strides in technology and inclusion, it's still difficult to learn another language, understand other customs and norms, connect with your new neighbours and break into the job market.

And for me, that's why I put this book together. People have told me before that I should write a book about the many stories I have from travelling. Many of them didn't make it into this book.

I wanted it to be something more than a collection of anecdotes, and to be useful for people in a similar situation as myself, an international student, a traveller, an entrepreneur.

It's my challenges, my triumphs, the tips I have learned, the tricks I have played and the advice I have received along the way.

It can be used as a blueprint on how to succeed in university.

It can be used as a guide on how to maximise your travel experience.

It can be used as a roadmap to build a business, nourish a network, bounce back after a failure, and forge your own version of success.

This book is many things.

But personally? I think it's my father's wisdom come to life. It's about giving back, being a good friend, seeking to help people and in return, achieving your own dreams.

It's not easy when you're a migrant to build a home away from home. But when you reflect on your values, your childhood passions, your idols, the people who inspire you and the people who support you, it becomes clearer what you need to do and how you need to achieve it.

I'll leave you with the words of my idol, Mahatma Gandhi: *If I have the belief I can do it, I shall surely acquire the capacity to do it even if I may not have it at the beginning.*

In my opinion, Gandhi was a genius.

Thanks for reading,

— *Nilesh Makwana*

About The Author

Nilesh Makwana is an Indian-Australian entrepreneur living and working in Perth, with his lovely wife Lene, a Norwegian artist.

He is the co-founder and CEO of illuminance Solutions, a National Technology Company and a Microsoft Global Partner for Social Impact. With his partner Vincent Lam, Nilesh has built a high-performing team of co-workers from 26 different countries, making it one of the most diverse workplaces in Australia.

When he is not working, Nilesh can be found partying with friends (but he is strictly no alcohol!) or playing cricket, tennis, swimming, or cycling. He is a vegetarian and a big fan of reggae music – particularly Bob Marley.

With his wife, Lene, Nilesh has established a NGO - Borderless Gandhi to promote Mahatma Gandhi's message of peace, equality and non-violence through various artistic reflections.

Nilesh has the honour of being an Auspire - Australia Day Council Ambassador and with his interactions with community members he inspires Australians to be more diverse and inclusive. In recognition of his many achievements, Nilesh has won many national and international awards.

Nilesh's first book, *Terminal 4 - An Entrepreneur's Journey from Bicycle to Business Class* takes readers from his childhood in India to his studies in the UK and Australia and his business ventures - all through the lens of a migrant.

www.nilesh.com